JESUS
SAVES

another one

Praise
God!

This is poetry work. Historical individuals and places and events are mentioned. Villages are actual name places. All other characters, locales, and accounts of events may be fictional and are entirely the product of the author's imagination, and any similarities are purely coincidental.

Published by arrangement with
Advanced Concept Design Books
Library of Congress Control Number
to be assigned
International Standard Book Number
ISBN 13: 978-1-965535-22-6?

For information, address

axlerod@peoplepc.com
rseibert@advancedconceptdesign.com
First paperback printing June 2026
Printed in the United States of America
First Edition June 2026 10 9 8 7 6 5 4 3 2 1

≡ thanks from my heart to ≡

Mike O'Brien and Alex Hinton Kuba
for every tattoo ever for forever,

Dani Bradeson for her wonderful rainbow
painting of my beautiful AppleJacks,
and Alberto Cruz with his somehow
perfect depictions of visualizing
my AppleJacks and me gazing up at
the multicolored Universe and then
us, flying together through it,

Elders Aaron, Cade, and Kelly
truly True Missionaries extraordinaire
and... nothing less than
life changers
my brothers in Christ
Bryan and Forrest
for bringing me home again. ♡

Praise God!

for my
eternal companions

AppleJacks
and
Haloʻd J.

forward

And there were also many other things that Jesus did, which if they were written one by one, I suppose that even the world itself could not contain the books that would be written. Amen.

-John 21:25 (NKJV)

↑

write of Christ;
how he is working
in our lives now
just like they did
"in Bible times". Just
as there is a record
of then, make a record
of now, because the
Bible itself would not
exist had there not
been writers writing
their record of Him.
write it.
write it.
write it.

Table of Contents

> = =

34 - when people ask if I am a Christian
35 - yes, I promise
36 - zero times zero times zero

Purple Church of Jesus
not-a-sermons

so let it be written…
Preach!

Mike O'Brien tattoo stencil:
Palm Sunday donkey Amir, carrying Ephesians 1:19

just breathe

eight
October 30, 2025
Return to the Root

nine
November 13, 2025
for our beautiful perrita Athena & every dog in the world, thank you

ten
November 27, 2025
finding lost gratitude

eleven
December 10, 2025
He found me!

twelve
December 11, 2025
Praise God!

thirteen
December 24, 2025
Happenstance, the Christmas Moth

fourteen
January 5, 2026
one more upheaval returns to earth

fifteen
January 12, 2026
in the name of Jesus Christ, amen.

sixteen
January 19, 2026
Jesus, Martin Luther King, & Shadrach together at Purple Church of Jesus

seventeen
February 2, 2026
God's Minneapolis Macrame

eighteen
February 26, 2026
Black History Month 2026

nineteen
March 12, 2026
Faith already knows to just keep on moving mountains

twenty
March 25, 2026
letting go; also, not ever letting go

twenty-one
April 3, 2026

remembering the potter's field

twenty-two
April 5, 2026
the immeasurable greatness

twenty-three
April 13, 2026
ain't going for naked emperors selling lies and fear

twenty-four
April 20, 2026
to know the love of Christ that surpasses knowledge

twenty-five
May 7, 2026
cross-legged floor puzzles with Jesus

twenty-six
May 11, 2026
humble donkeys carrying Greatness

together with Mom, on the train to Temple Square at Christmas
Forrest's scripture
Bryan's testimony
Elder Cade and Elder Aaron's testimonies
Christ statue photo: Elder Kelly Johnson
You Are Beautiful
Alberto Cruz drawing: flying through the Multicolored Universe
BFFFE means FFE
Dani Bradeson painting: my AppleJacks
Purple Church of Jesus goes outdoors
Palm Sunday re-imagined

Mike O'Brien tattoo stencil: JESUS SAVES
Alberto Cruz drawing: AppleJacks and pastor toddymanners

…in the name of Jesus Christ, amen
God created dog smiles

The How
is Holy

> = =

they want you to think
(they being those with the most
power), that greater-than is
not equal to equal but,
if you look,
very, very closely you can
see between two who have
equal
direct eye contact while talking
of just things
unrelated, maybe,
not even having anything
to do when coming to
establishing establishment's
push-throughs;
those, all-important
non-negotiations of placement
and place
in silence,
taking place unidirectionally
between

two sets of unequal ayes
in the name of betterment for
everybody; their commodity,

when what is born
equal
only loses its value
when we sell it.

5.18.26

ADHD prayer

I love you, God. Thank you. Thank you
for this new day. Thank you for being,
for being here with me, and for me
knowing that you and me are always
truly connected; thank you for that,
in a way that I know that
being here with you in all ways
fills me with every sense of purpose,
direction and necessity
in and on your pathway of love... is
all that I will ever need... to help
get me through this world's nonsense
while remaining
brave enough to touch
life's beauty. Thank you. Thank you
for all of that and for everything.
I give all of myself to you, knowing
that you know exactly
what to do... with me;
thank you, God. I love you, God. Thank you.

arms up in praise

...in surrender...

swimming in love

... submerged...

with a falling off

backwards eyes closed...

... then caught once

again

by

you.

comfort happens.
I would like to say that
you knew that but that is not
helpful; just more harmful
when you knew
everything to do with that
moot point.
so I will remain
mute once again while
I patiently watch
you
begin to let go
of those burdensome
toljasos that were
never of any use to you
anyhow. seeing you
trust not having to
absolve anyone
or anything, being
dissoluable sutures
that just know for you,
your wounds have healed
somehow; and now
it's ok to feel
comfort again.

covered

when Jesus said

"It is finished."

He did not mean that

_we_

were done.

crossing no-man's land

someone
built

an electrified fence
between God and me,

but when I looked
only to God,

He knocked it down

and I became
ELECTRIFIED

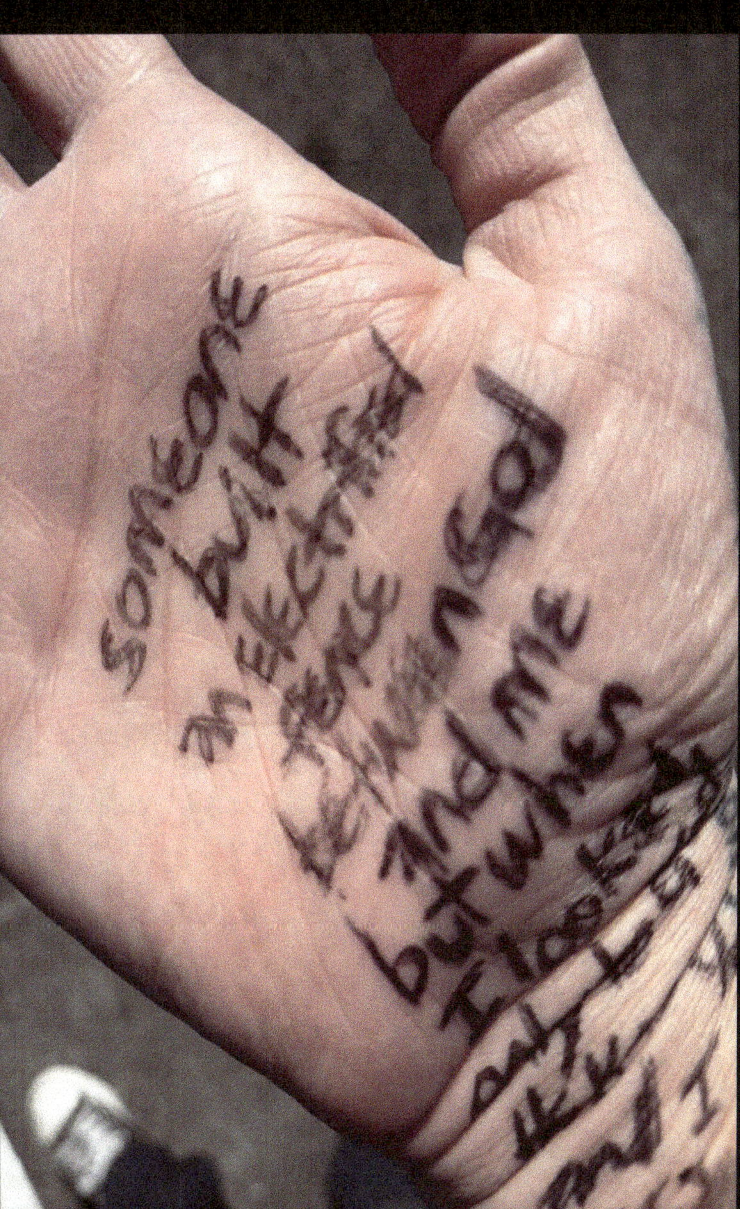
someone
built
an electrified
fence
between God
and me
but when
I looked

and me
but when
I looked
only to
and I
became
here

Divine contact

phantom limbs have their own
universally unseen universes
the inside-out
silent accompaniment of spirit
so very persistent
although
not without unresolvable pain
or plain
itchiness of what had been
chopped off or lost, just
the baptism of fire; that's all
here, bearing gifts,
God's own version of being
one, or all three
kings bringing treasure to purpose
establishing simultaneous warmth
and relevance
in every direction of paying
attention to His true Spirit
confirming this Holy
conversation of ours is
no longer porous.

do not get caught up
in a dance
with confusion. there is
no absolute purpose
in figuring on figuring out
anything while
you are in faith;
without any asinine needs
for reason to begin with that
constant tug of wars' unpaid
wages. consciousness prays about
getting its lights punched
into exxes
by way of subconsciousness playing
footsies with
awakening what will
please, pretty please,
turn every inch of groundwork
into blazing
destruction.

dream Kevin

slow dancing in our bedroom,
Kevin with his shirt off and
six-pack abs, laughing loudly
with his face up to the sky
when I surprised him
during our favorite flavor of quiet
time together; our temples
find each other's place where
the sharp-cornered skull-puzzle edges
match in that one spot,
fit together
because
they were made to, then
nuzzle. that moment is one
where we both know without speaking
to stay quiet
for as long as it lasts
except for this time, when
I broke the unspoken rule;
tongue stuck
with a quick dart into his ear, then
so much exquisite
unleashed laughter.

fine print

it's lost somewhere
in the fine print,
or maybe, this time, it's found
by reading just the made-up
stuff between the lines, but
it must be in there,
somewhere,
because it happens all of the time.
Jesus, saying
forsake all to follow me
more often than not becoming
the one to be
forsaken.

grace notes

every single day
when you take the time
to pay ^ attention to
sufficient
all of that
already-beautiful
everything that keeps on
materializing
once and forever right
here in the middle of
just showing up for it; while
allowing all of the rest
to finally become
immaterial.

for AJ

gratitude bingo

so much
of what
I never thought I would see
is
now
right there in front of me
on my very own
never on my own
gratitude bingo card.
thank you, God. ♡

2826

grow
anyway

Then Jesus said to His disciples,

"If anyone desires to come after Me,
let him deny himself, and take up his cross,
and follow Me.
For whoever desires to save his life
will lose it, but whoever loses his life for
My sake will find it.
For what profit is it
to a man if he gains
the whole world,
and loses his own soul?
Or, what will a man give in exchange for

his soul?"

-Matthew
NKJV
16:24-26

last night, I dreamed
I was seeing
dozens of fireflies,
the first of the year, floating
between twilight branches
while music from where
souls are born
began to descend all around
where I stood;
fresh... giant-soft
snowflake notes landing on
miniature mountaintop ears
learning how listening
to music,
heard only through quiet eyes
settles

living in the immeasurable

this understanding has happened before,
when I came to see unseen beauty
in everything;
everywhere that I went, it was
already there; all everywhere.
so much beauty filling my eyes
with all of its obstinate molecules;
converting windows, portals gone
past any continuing need
for moot exponentials of flowery curtains.
molting into this obvious
beauty submarine
means establishing
a whole new set of built-ins. yes;
reinvention hard-knocking with
unsolicited insistence.
this is that
same
transformational
understanding
of no longer having that long known
hyperventilation heaving with valiant failures
to capture...
to contain... more;
immeasurable.

121825

living
proof

right here
where there is

no
either/or

of truth
and freedom

with Jesus

always
and already
being

everything.

look at that halo...

...as a portal to be

where

hearing seeing and speaking with the Holy Spirit requiring FAITH jumping off from having to understand anything first. This 100x is the first and essential, foundational manner to be living by FAITH; that makes the blind to see and the lame to walk.

adequate access to
one's

unconditional, complicated
allowance of love
obtained
through
accessing allowance

to
release

my own.

no shadow

you know when
you have been
saved by the grace
of JESUS

and you cannot hide
the fact
that while following
Him

as He lives
inside your heart

the day will arrive when

you won't know if

you have lost your shadow.

not knowing
what's next
≠
done.

...and on the day of rest
the Lord said "let there be
dog smiles," knowing,
to anyone who had been paying
attention to details
up to this point, the point
would have been known that
God had already created
all of the dogs in the world
earlier in the week, but,
in fact, possibly the first but-
something of anything in history
God had seen ... in His creation...
creating consternation...
...there was more to <u>this</u> <u>being</u>
being considered completion.
So, on that first,
most famous day of rest,
God created dog smiles;
and God could see
that it was good
and God rested.

ours is the home where
mountains move.
where no one knew
what miracle for who was
inches away from walking
through a doorway
where ten minutes before that
impossible,
freedom didn't exist and
hadn't, as such, for so many
invisible
longtimes... n o b o d y
even remembered
what
mountains look like; seeing them
materialize
while we climb them. greatness,
be what is,
already.

for my brothers in Christ:
Bryan, Forrest, and Shawn

please tell me: ___ . ___ . ___ . ___

what was
the very first word
Jesus
said upon His resurrection
when He returned,
and then

think about what we
must never forget to
do; always.

Matthew 28:9

Sasquatch love letter

Dear Jesus,
thank you for finding me
way out here; as some would
say "way out there," but not
You.
You found me
way out here; right here.
And when
I stopped being afraid to start
loving you out loud again, You
immediately showed me, even
in all of my sasquatchiness, You
never ever stopped
loving me with that same
everything
You've
always
got; the same way
—I know we are one—
'cause that is how true love is.

stolen valor

to wear the uniform
falsely
representing oneself as
having served
one's country
honorably, wearing medals
baring dishonorable
false witness
in order to gain
unearned favor
through imagined shortcuts
of lies
the same way
in the name of
the cross
worn just
prominently enough to provide
quick onramps to televised
self-righteousness
saying believe all of this;
'cause Jesus.

stoner Jesus

if people still threw
physical sticks and stones
at people they just couldn't
get along with, if they ever used to,
which, don't get me wrong,
some still do; who is to say that
rather than attacking with words
there wouldn't be carts filled
with rental rocks, surrounding
every U.S. American town square.
Now,
think about any stoner
who you ever knew, or maybe
that stoner was or is
you. then ask
yourself or a friend who isn't busy
dragging their knuckles, if all of this
Jesus stuff
from 'back then' was the same way
today, did Jesus talk more
like someone who would throw down
every 'other' with fists full of stones
or, did he speak more
like someone
who just wants to sit with you while
sharing
a few sticky bowls.

surfing with Jesus

they/them being those invisible
people who, sometimes, are
smart about some stuff, say
the best way to survive
becoming stuck
in a deep pit of
quick sand
is to just stop
struggling
for one or two small
counterintuitive-as-f***
moments, allowing yourself enough time
to slowly float up again and rest
on your back,
breathing evenly for long enough
to watch the clouds floating
along above you...then roll-along
off to the side of what
you had been certain was the most
final swallowing of you; still here
escaping in time to also see Jesus
standing on water
with a surfboard for two,
saying "alright, brother, swells-to-be-done;
now c'mon".

survival of there
—·— being·——·——
no more distance left
between saving face here, and
can't combine; spirit,

without

what is

physical

in

com

pati

bili

ty

'cause really
just
anybody
could...

bear witness to this rediscovery.

≡ tactile ≡

@toddymanners;

where tactile was not, before.

this is what it means
to praise God

this is what it means
to honor the blood
of our brother,
Jesus

this is what it means
to believe
in what
you know you can
believe in faith

this is what is
already here for you.

My Halo'd J;
my Jesus with

two hands

envisioning certainty's
thorns to teepees
isn't easy
at first stomach-flutter
letting go of what
you thought you saw for sure
to be
all stickery either
turned-out or left on your own,
becoming, on approach,
still-not-stopping who or
they-what-grow into our
first
traveling encampment

5526

the unsubtle anarchy of prayer

I believe that I must be
the very last person on earth
to fully realize none of this is,
terrible, or not, just
a movie trailer; boasting of
unimaginable brokenness
scooped-up and shaped into breakthroughs
in two hours or less. like spending
half of the day walking through
public spaces with no one, ever
waking me up to the fact that
I had a bat in the cave
the whole time and maybe, I should
find a paper napkin, or tissue, or
at the very least
a discreet dig for it. But no,
I have been left cruelly alone
to find, and figure out
all of that on my own; that
all of this... is... really happening.
So, this time,

don't leave me hanging again,
just tell me...
what am I supposed to do,
discretely or not, with
all of these super-delicate, yet,
absolutely true visions that keep on
happening
when I close my eyes,
with respect, in prayer. Sheer
unbelievable anarchy to be seeing
what isn't there, whenever
never even asking for all of that
open source code with no
language... for any of it.
rudeness in reverse,
to realize after-the-fact,
I had never even thought to say
please; thankfully, this time,
I already know that this is also
not a movie trailer:

eyes-closed-darkness
breaking apart into
it's-not-too-smart
to stare at the sun like that
...brightness...

everyone's visions begin this way;
am I right?... then, finding...

a simple wedding ring floats
like heaven's slow settling sediment;
my direction being right
in its tumbling flightpath when
the whole person-of-me becomes
a tiny, striped bead,
woven into a chair's
wide right armrest right next to
thousands of others'
tiny striped beads
woven everywhere,
across every surface
of this
unwearying-chair
when, suddenly,

my right arm is... somehow...
a regular human arm again,
just-in-time for

a hand from nowhere

I've seen before
making
this vision tactile;
bringing me forward by the forearm.

the pure anarchy of purposefulness
could not have been imagined as
arriving so

gently as we go...
eyes opened; and here...

we begin.

when people ask
if I am a Christian,
there is

no automatic answer

(from me, at least)
because
in my understanding of spirit
and experience,
there is sometimes a difference
between being
a Christian in name and
being reborn
in Christ. sometimes
people are both. Sometimes though,
people have taken His name
without showing what it means,
without even speaking (for some)
to be one with Him;
leaving a trail of spiritual abuse
in their "don't
call me woke" wake. So I ask you to
understand, that
when you ask me if

I am a Christian,
I will raise my hands high into the sky
in absolute affirmation with the
integrity of all of my being
best described as doing
my best
to be
a true follower of Jesus Christ.
He is the truth
and the light
and the life and
I will follow Him
wherever I go.
Thank you, God.
I love You I praise You I thank You;
I worship You
and
I will follow You
wherever You want me to go.

Praise Jesus.
Praise His Holy Name.

I love you, Jesus, with all of my heart,
for every particle and part of
forever,

Amen.

---

anytime
my beautiful Soledad
holds my face
with both of her hands

our eyes locked in contact, then
very gently, intentionally
vibrates my whole head
through my cheeks while

she speaks in that quieted tone
that means listen to me
right now. I know to listen

with my heart and both of my ears;
to this, because it is so. That is
my long way of saying yes,
I promise,

Purple Church of Jesus will continue.

(in case of emergency, remember:)

zero times zero times zero

how many
perfect people are in the world
right now, including
all of the people you trust
the very most
both in person and as a position in
modern society's assignments of role,
from the Pope to your mother and
how many people, do you think
existed or will exist
from the very beginning of time
to its finish,
other than Jesus, who had nothing
to ask or receive forgiveness
for, whenever and forever included
in that number; plus one more
time of
how many people,
out of everybody,
could not possibly, ever

be forgiven.

@toddymanners

Preach!

Ephesians 1:19

JUST
BREATHE

Return to the Root
October 30, 2025

Welcome to Purple Church of Jesus, and thank you for being here. This is important to me, and I'm really trying to do something here that I hope is effective, and I really appreciate you showing up for me to do this.
So, there's this new song that is in my mind that I'll just read the first few lines of, or try to sing, and I'll just start, just raw, acapella:

I speak Jesus - by Charity Gayle

If you ever get a chance to sing it, especially with a group, it's got quite a few wonderful crescendos that feel great to sing and be a part of. So, I wanted to sing that song starting today's welcome to Purple Church of Jesus, and talking about Jesus being our BFFFE. While getting ready to write today's not-a-sermon, I was sitting here in our Purple Church, listening to music, starting my day with prayer and meditation, feeling that it's important to start the day by having a conversation with that one connection that I plan on spending the whole day with, one day at a time, loving when the day starts that way, trying to remember to start the day that way every day, feeling our language speak like intertwining heartbeats, getting our rhythm together right cause whatever happens throughout the day, knowing that it could be one of those anything-goes kind of days, no matter what, slow or fast, or all erratic all day, we're dance partners.

This room that we're in, Purple Church of Jesus, feels like a living room to me. And while I'm here, no matter what kind of nonsense and fear mongering could be happening outside those doors, I remember that I am living in this moment, in this living room of a church, and that God's got me. No matter what's burning or bouncing around, or breaking, maybe outside or inside of my head, in this living space I remember that I'm doing alright, right now, in this moment, and that I can continue with whatever it is that God has asked of me today, which is basically just to show up and let Him steer the wheel, while trying to not behave like a terrible backseat driver, worrying about traffic and road hazards the whole way. I don't know about you, but somedays if feels like things get a little bit more super-sized than just another one of those "God's got me in his hands" days, and I start having one of those "I'll bet that I'm starting to be a real handful" kind of days instead, like the day feels like it's just taking another direction like it's sparking out sideways from upside-down elbows feeling like going the wrong way on a detoured locals-only one-way street with its foot heavy on the "so what" gas pedal, saying "please God, it's me again, asking you sincerely to help me to not sabotage my whole life while trying to just be here, breathing today, unable to be completely present, or present at all, because of becoming too exhausted by the enormity of my right-now thoughts right now, gonna have to ask, please God, help me get through this brain-freezing juggle to stop, or to at least go in slo-mo again, toot-sweet if you don't mind, using a phrase from a happy song that just landed in my head, but only if you're not already too busy, pretty please, and all-the-way thank you."

Being pulled outta rushing currents of overwhelming thoughts; too much importance on important stuff making us unable to do anything at all, sometimes making all of that become a "pretty-please, God." I know that God must have way more important stuff to do, but hey, if what they've taught us is true about God being omnipotent and omnipresent, that includes omniscience with that too. He's already gonna be aware of the situation anyway, and will wait while we run around in circles, using up all of our energy and air again, letting people know that we can't breathe. If you're a person like me, you 100% do that to yourself by nature of wanting to be a part of, and take care of, one hundred thousand things all at once and in the ten seconds that are left between task numbers 399 and 400, figuring out what you can do with that open time-slot of 399-1/2. Next thing you know, if you're doing it like I do, 399-1/2 equals being incapable of doing anything at all, and even that one-most-important-thing-of-all begins looking like too-many-everythings-all-at-once; and my mind needs to close up shop again for a little while, spending a little bit of time on my own, here at Purple Church.

It has to be helpful, to get that back on-track when I need to, to think that this repeat behavior would change someday, and that I would learn to try something new. Time and time again, there I go, doing that same hard-smacking belly-flop straight into another lack-of-time-management whirlpool again, running around like a programmable vacuum cleaner all charged up without a floor-plan or a motherboard while I'm jam-smashing all of the buttons. Although, the ordinary struggles that I have in my sixties look a whole lot different than the ones that I had in my twenties and thirties and forties, that feeling of churning is the same; the solution to it is the same too. Jesus saying, "Come unto me, ye who are weary, for my yoke is easy and my burden is light." Sometimes I ask myself "where is this light burden that you're talking about, Jesus? Because, sometimes, it keeps on feeling like it's too much, too big, too overwhelming, and too late to effectively resist the tidal wave of whatever-it-is." And, in whatever decade of life I'm currently in, it's headed straight for me again; even when it's all just too much of the good stuff…and one… two… three… here we go under…trying to remember to do that one thing that we automatically do over six-hundred million times during any ordinary human lifespan: breathe.

Just that. Just breathe; and do it one more time, taking your time. And again, breathe.

Remembering to do this isn't as easy as it would seem, 'cause, how do you ever stop when it appears to be that the only solution is to go faster. "Come unto me, ye who are weary, for my yoke is easy and my burden is light." One of my favorite phrases is, if you can't find enough time to meditate for 10-minutes a day, then meditate for 15-minutes a day. How is that even possible? While, at the same time, of course. There's got to be a way to say "enough" sometimes, even about all of the good stuff that will always be sitting right in front of us, blinking right at us, that we will always want to do start-to-finish, feeling like we've got it all under control the whole time. If you are people who can relate to that; it's something that I do to myself over and over again.

I was having one of my several OCD moments of the day, when I left my house to do something, I don't remember what, with the GPS on, telling me exactliy how to get there and exactly how long it would take to get there too, when that OCD kicked-in and said to me "Hey! What about this or that or this or that so you'd better turn around and go home for a moment to be sure of… or to get… whatever. In the meantime, with the GPS still running, it became very confusing for that GPS voice, that had become very busy with telling me to turn back around so many times that it finally just started repeating "Return to the route", pronouncing it "rOOt" rather than "rOWte" for some reason. I don't know where people decided to say it one way or the other, but there it was, saying "return to the root, return to the root, return to the root," probably to the beat of a Red Hot Chili Peppers song that was likely playing at the same time; "return to the root, return to the root." Relentless; it wouldn't just let it go of it, saying "return to the root" so many times, without even having a root that I'd be paying attention to at all; it got stuck in my mind. I thought of a root-system, like an inverted hand, burrowing into the ground in order to gather water and nutrients. I thought "That's it. I get to have five things as 'my roots', just like my hand; five things. If it doesn't fit within one of those five things, at least for now, sorry about that, 'cause right now I've just gotta return to the root; five things, that's it, easy, and in order:

one: God; including everything within that that we've got together, whatever He asks me to do.
two: 12-step recovery; every day.
three: my family; siempre juntos y siempre cresciendo
four: my friends; irreplaceable
five: taking enough whatever quiet-time looks like for me; today.

Five things. "For my yoke is easy and my burden is light" doesn't mean nothing; it just doesn't mean everything. My great big giant sleigh, full of ego-and-denial-and-automatic-opposition starts resembling the one full of stolen packages on "How the Grinch Stole Christmas"; just about to topple over a cliff while my heart shivers for a minute, thinking "I'd better whittle-it-back to those five things right-quick, remembering, "return to the root."

I won't ever forget going for a long walk, with one of my big brothers, way, way back in my teenager days. We'd go for these super long, super great walks when he would see that I was getting all tangled-up, and I'd get to ask all of my big questions, like whether there really is a God or not, and does any of this matter. And he would always have the right answers to help put my mind at ease about all of that complicated stuff, usually by talking to me the same way that Jesus like to teach; through parables. My big brother would always have some parable that he could come up with on-the-fly, just by looking around at wherever we were walking around at the time, and making a super applicable story about that one thing, whatever it was. That is an incredible gift that he has, being able to so naturally do this; being able to see the lessons and guidance all around us, just by looking around and seeing what was right in front of us. I still do that today; nearly every day, without even thinking about it, because of him showing me how to look at things when I was a kid. Thanks for that, my big brother. During one of those long walks, we were trodding along a fast-moving, shallow canal, in the off-road foothills of a great big mountain. Another perfect day outside, to be talking and taking a walk with my big brother, listening to what he had to say about complicated stuff when he suddenly stopped walking and got quiet for a minute. I stood there next to him, wondering what was up. He said "Look in the water, there next to us, and tell me what you see." I could see that there was a small, rusted-up anchor, sitting solid on the floor of the canal while water was rushing all around it. Who knows how or why it was sitting there in a canal, in the foothills of a great big mountain, but there it was, firmly stuck in place. Without saying anything, my big brother took off his shoes and socks, walked into the water, picked up the anchor, walked back out of the water, and put the anchor on the dirt trail that we had been walking on. He said, "That anchor is you, stopping and not wanting to move along with the currents rushing by; still kind of stuck there, unable to move." He said, "Me, climbing into that water, lifting up that anchor and bringing it to shore, allowing it time to dry-off again, just breathing while thinking about 'what was that, that I was so stuck-in' is what Jesus does for us; lifting us up when we're stuck, bringing us to a place of being able to dry-off again, carrying us to solid land, then, standing-by and with us, as we learn the lessons of what was, and what just happened. This is what Jesus does for us, especially when we think that we are stuck." The story that my big brother told me that day stayed with me even to now; whole decades later.

Even as I still, somehow, and sometimes even a lot of times, get stuck somewhere in my brain, whether it's in life's anxieties, air-depleting depression, much too complicated thoughts, or all of the above, that rushing water, carrying with it all of the stuff that I could never comprehend or know what to do with other than to stop on all-stuck-again for a minute or two before asking "Hey Jesus, sorry to bug you again, could you give me a lift?" And, there it is, and here we are, remembering to meditate for fifteen minutes this time instead of complaining about not having ten.

I love the Bible story of Jesus walking on water. And I love how, as I was writing today's not-a-sermon, this is the Bible story that came to mind. Jesus being able to walk on water, and us thinking that we either already are, or are at least trying; sometimes even quietly demanding that of ourselves, to be as perfect as we can be. Whether it's because of our insecurities or the flip-side of that same coin, our insatiable ego, or if it's because of truly wanting to follow his example, there we are, thinking that we can, or at least that we are trying, to walk on water too, while Jesus stands there, watching us wrestle with our struggle as we keep on learning more stuff.

It was after those walks with my big brother, that I was out on my own, had been going through what was a heavy enough depression for me to juggle-around with finding what the best suicide method would be for me. …drowning. I was living near the ocean coast at the time, and I decided that the best way for me to go would be to swim into the ocean as far as I could go, until I was exhausted; so exhausted that if I changed my mind about it I wouldn't have enough energy left to swim back to the shore. Thank you, God, that I didn't go further with that thought, and that I somehow found myself in a program of recovery that helped me learn how to live one day at a time; taking a few steps to learn how to begin doing what I could never figure out how to do. I think back again, to the Bible story of Jesus walking on the water, seeing Peter struggle and begin to sink, and then calmly walking over to him as He calmed the storms around them, reminding him with His outreached hand that, although he still had further to go, growing in his faith, right here in this moment, His capable hand was reaching out to him, offering His help to pull him right back up out of the water again, living for another day of learning to strengthen his faith as he found his purpose.

And here's me, years and years after thoughts of having that long swim, actually old… HAH! Hearing the "see a need, fill a need" call to start-up Purple Church of Jesus; doing my best to do just that. Trying to help fill a need for LGBTQIA+ humans specifically, and as I am finding out, anybody who has gone through, or who is still going through spiritual abuse, being left to believe by "the-true-believers" that it's better for everyone if they're to be left disconnected from God, for any one of a hundred thousand of their fearful-judgment reasons, those hateful voices can be brutal, whether the voices are "innies or outies" and;

Jesus here, saying, "Come unto me… for my burden is light." Us, learning to say, "ok… show us how to do that." He's quietly smiling for a minute, then, sure enough, there it goes again; return to the root, return to the root, return to the root.

I know that, the fact that I'm here, doing Purple Church of Jesus, is evidence of the strength of my testimony of Jesus; that never left me. No matter what I was going through, no matter how far I strayed, no matter what struggles I had, no matter how much hatred I felt towards me and toward others, until it was everything around me, no matter how much I wanted to sabotage and destroy myself and everything around me; still being here today, still learning the same lessons in a different way, because of wanting to take on all of the stuff around me and having to say, "ok (counting on my fingers… 1, 2, 3, 4, 5) these are the five that I can do today," and then ask Jesus for help.

I had kind of a funny situation, earlier, when I was trying to find my glasses, 'cause I needed to write something, a little bit more, and I was thinking "where are my glasses, where are my glasses, where are my glasses?" And you know, that anxiety, it's just right outside the door for me. I don't know about other people who just sit like they're in a jacuzzi living life the easy way all day. I mean, I can get through a day, and I can be doing alright, but sometimes that anxiety, or the depression, is not too far away and I need several reminders through the day. Like I said, I don't want to be "too much of a handful" to God. I want to be able to ask for Him, but I don't want to be too-much-too-much of a handful. But yeah, I can be having a peaceful day and, all of a sudden I can't find my glasses and I'm all "well, where are they?" Wandering through the house, wandering through the house, wandering through the house; "where would I have put them, where would I have put them?" It's a thing, being like, "I got this." I was talking with some friends last night, about "I got this." Thinking of it like, the church-going person's equivalent of faith; the God-person's equivalent of "I got this" kinda the same thing as "hold my beer…" the last thing you say before you doing something stupid and terrible. Thinking "I got this" is not going to be the solution when I'm in a struggle. Remembering though, to ask for help, to pray, to pray to God, saying "I need some help. Please God, I don't know if it's ego or fear or whether it's doing a lot of everything that would make me not automatically think of reaching out and asking for help when I'm in that kind of a space, but, for me to say "I got this" is the same as someone saying "here, hold my beer" right before they blow their hand off with fireworks. So, I thought "Where are my glasses, where are my glasses, where are my glasses? You know what? I think that I put them down on the couch when I was saying a prayer for help; asking for guidance with what to talk about. I think that I put them right down on the couch right next to where I had my prayers." I walked over there, and there's my glasses. I thought "that's really cool, thanks God, for reminding me that I had remembered, earlier, to ask for help." I thought, 'that was really cool.' I don't know why it is that there's not an automatic response. Kind of like when I was talking about breathing, how it's something that we do millions of times in our life, and when going through situations sometimes that's all that we need to remember to do, is to breathe, just for a minute, or a few, in quiet meditation. It's the same with reaching out to God for help. Sometimes we'll just be spinning around in circles with our hair on fire when all that we needed to do was to remember to kneel down and ask for help, have that trust in God, and to give the things to him that we can; remembering, return to the root.

I'm grateful that we have this space. I'm grateful for the things that it brings me to be thinking about as I think about what would be beneficial to others both in the good stuff and in the all-of-the-everything stuff. So, thank you, and I love you, and I'm grateful for you and everyone here. I almost brought my AppleJacks with me here this time, but I will for sure bring him next time.

Thank you Jesus, thank you God, thank you all who have brought so much beauty and so much love and strength into my life, all of the people in my life who I am grateful for. I couldn't do this alone; I'm grateful to know that. I say these things in the name of Jesus Christ, amen.

Purple Church of Jesus
greatness
greatness
be what is
♡ for everyone for forever ♡

For Our Beautiful Athena & Every Dog in the World,
Thank You
November 13, 2025

Come Sail Away - by Styx

Welcome to Purple Church of Jesus where everyone is welcome, including our dogs; every dog, probably even more than any people. And, speaking of dogs, one of our beautiful dogs, little Athena, after living her full, happy life, went to the Multicolored Universe last week. She had been rescued as a puppy, by a friend of mine, from a gas station while my friend was filling-up her truck's gas tank, when she noticed our soon-to-be little brindle-boxer puppy, Athena, who hadn't even been given her name yet, sitting in the bed of another person's truck who was also getting a fill-up at the same time. My friend struck up a conversation with the other person, and, come to find out, little Athena and her puppy brother, who was sitting in the truck bed right next to her, were both on their way to the pound, where they'd probably only have three-or-so days for someone to adopt them before that-would-be-the-end of their short story altogether. The guy my friend was talking to said "you can take them both if you want, otherwise they're headed straight from here to the pound." My friend scooped them both up, and found homes for them both. Athena; with her life story suddenly redirected, immediately became a member of our Happy Animal Family for the next several years, and after living her full happy life with us, has now gone on to join our other Happy Animal Family members who have gone on before her; all of them saving a human-shaped spot for me to join them someday, 'cause there's no other version of heaven where I'd rather be… if not there, then just forget about it.

There's a poem that I wrote, a while ago, which I made into two
word-for-word identical versions, title and everything; one of them
as if written by:
-a dog at an animal shelter

and the other as if written by:
-a young street hustler in Hollywood

poem called "stray"

it's ok if I never
find a home.
just feed me,
let your eyes
tell me that I'm
beautiful, and
don't kill me
while I'm waiting
to be found.

Heavy way to start my not-a-sermon, I know, but I wanted to give a moment to show love and respect for our little Athena, and for all of the dogs in the world; who truly end up rescuing us.

(meditation time for all of the dogs in the world)

I started this not-a-sermon with an attempt at a song that I love from way-way-way back when I first discovered music to be a very effective escape; headphones on, lying on my back on the living room floor with a throw pillow behind my head; eyes closed and I'd be gone. This song came from the first record that I ever bought, and every song on that record could take me there with my headphones on.

While driving around this week, thinking about my not-a-sermon for this second-iteration of our, "every-second" Thursday-of-the-month Purple Church pit-stop, right after retrieving our beautiful Athena's ashes from our veterinarian, I saw a bright yellow patio chair, in sort of a stuck-in-a-toppling-over position; left abandoned in the middle of a hilly-field of very high wild-grass. Also seeing nearby, a small group of flowers, all on their own, tiny as could be in that whole great big field; tiny flowers which also happened to be the very same bright yellow color as that abandoned, halfway-toppling-over chair just a few feet away, while going up the hill from the veterinarian's office. I'm 100% not kidding; everything that I saw was exactly like that. Of course, being one of those kinda-weird-in-a-weird-way type of humans, I pulled the car over, stopped, and stepped outside of my car to be present with that moment for a little while. I do stuff like that when it feels like it's a random, unexpected moment like that. Maybe weird for anyone else, but when I see stuff like that it tells me to stop, pay attention to that moment, and let my brain breathe with it for a while. If that ever happens for you, I personally think that's a cue to follow-through with those instincts, so I hope that you do.

Later, that very same day, one of my big brothers let me know that he and his wife were on their way to see that same band play, whose song I tried to play at the very beginning of this not-a-sermon. In addition to that band creating the first record that I ever bought, going to see that same band perform live had been the first concert that my big brother and I had ever gone to, and we'd gone there together with his wife-to-be at the time. The two of them still being together all of these years later; seeing that show back then, while all of us were still teenagers. I like to hold onto great memories like that, to help fill in the cracks that sometimes happen while I'm going through the super-sad-stuff, like already having to say "see you soon, my beautiful little perrita" to my beautiful Athena this week.

Thinking of that one, famous song of theirs, along with the abandoned-mid-toppling chair and bright yellow flowers growing next to it that I had seen earlier in the day, had my head steering into the direction of this week's not-a-sermon.

As the rest of the week settled in, as I had expected but had hoped wouldn't happen as badly as it usually does, the deep depression over our beautiful Athena moving-on settled right in, and I thought to myself, maybe this isn't the best time to write this week's not-a-sermon; maybe I should cancel it for this week, and wait until I'm able to write something that is at least sorta-all-happy-again.

And, just like what happens so predictably, every time that I experience a big loss of someone who I love, right from the very core of me to the core of who they are too, all of the joy that we had together feels like it's gone forever and I inevitably begin to wonder, "why couldn't I have been the one that flew up from that toppling-over chair rather than my beautiful doggie; instead, me being the one who is still rooted here; randomly-growing bright yellow flowers; well, purple flowers in my case. A perfectly sunshiny day, as beautiful of a day as you could imagine, while still thinking how much longer until I can get yanked up into the sky too, leaving a toppled-over, primary-colored patio chair behind;

turning to prayer and meditation, to scriptures, to writing, to staying connected with my people, with my routines, doing one-day-at-a-time once again the way that it's worked a whole bunch of times before, even when it feels like it might not work this time. Not waiting to arrive at pretty-happy, before feeling what's real while on the way there.

Jeremiah: 29:11
For I know the thoughts that I think towards you, says the Lord; thoughts of peace and not of evil, to give you a future, and a hope.

Isaiah 43:18-19
Behold, I will do a new thing. Now it shall spring forth; shall you not know it? I will even make a road in the wilderness and rivers in the desert.

…and then, sure enough, one that says to me "pay attention to this" from Revelation 21:5
Then, he who sat on the throne said, "Behold, I make all things new." And he said until me, "<u>Write</u>, for these words are true and faithful."

In other words, "Not yet. Light a candle.
Let yourself cry when you need to, as much as you need to, and…"

who knows…
what's next for those of us who are still here, always arrives without bothering to ring the doorbell, it just comes on in…
maybe those bright yellow flowers were left behind, still rooted next to the tipped-over chair, still growing there for exactly the right time to feed some, lost, hungry creature that gets to go… "mmmm, yummy" for a minute on their path, munching along to wherever is next for them.

When it ain't time yet, it can sometimes take a whole field's worth of flowers of saying together, "Hey, it ain't time yet. There's still lots and lots of bees and butterflies out here who will be looking for us."

From last week's not a sermon, I talked about the scripture when Jesus said: "I am the truth and the life; he who believeth in me, though he were dead, yet shall he live," and then, remembering, of course, "return to the root. Return to the root." Leaving the "Why?" of that up to Him is sometimes, for me at least, the <u>biggest</u> act of faith that there is; just showing up for it today, <u>with that same faith</u> that we talk about during all of our 'over-the-top' happier days; leaving all of the answers to that gigantic, one-word question of '<u>Why</u>' up to God; not worrying about it, 'cause just like always, it always arrives and will arrive again, usually after forgetting about waiting for it to happen, with all of our… "are we there yet? are we there yet?"… just keep on capturing all of those delicious nutrients through these flower roots of ours… that the sunshine, the earth, and the rain keep on delivering, moving 24-hours-at-a-time worth of

forward…

finding sanctuary…

…like this physical spot, our Purple Church of Jesus, has turned out to be for me this week. Yep, I've stopped by here a few times lately, in the middle of the day with my puppy AppleJacks, sometimes just for the pure escape of a nap, and while I had been sleeping on the floor here at Purple Church, with my dog AppleJacks, listening to some easy going music because this living room church is a sanctuary that's perfect for that - when I "woke up in the dream" during one of those naps, still right here in dream-

Purple-Church, while actually still asleep and dreaming with everything exactly as it had been before, except for the dream-fact that my dog AppleJacks was no longer here with me. I became frantic about it, and, still in the dream, I got up from the dream-floor, looked all over, went out the front dream-door and kept on looking for my AppleJacks but he was nowhere around, which stressed me out <u>so much worse</u>, to the point that the worry in my dream became palpable enough that it woke me up for real and, whaddya know, I was still right here lying on the floor next to my puppy AppleJacks while the music was still playing; so grateful to be present, and here with him again, just like before.

Song: Suddenly - Xanadu soundtrack - Olivia Newton John
(…about giving it all to God.)

I do believe that the experiences I talked about at the beginning of this not-a-sermon, happening all together during that one-same-day, sometimes happen in clusters like that, giving us a chance to group them together, into a new constellation of a thought, like a music chord; or maybe just noticing the fact that that constellation already exists, is already in place right there; seeing the story that they make together has always existed, like hearing the notes of a familiar song chord all playing together, saying I'm thinking about you, right now, with this song-chord-vibration while you're thinking about me.

When I saw that "raptured" bright yellow chair, toppled post-rapture, right next to the staying-planted-right-here-for-right-now, group of bright yellow flowers, while bringing my beautiful Athena's ashes home with me I was thinking "still here with those flowers… still something to do… surrendering to it for today, dear God; grateful for the time that we have."

The next morning, while having time in prayer and meditation, kneeling next to my bed in the dark, my morning mind-fog found itself nudging towards thoughts about migrating butterflies, and I thought to myself "I know this feeling. This is what it feels like when another poem is about to happen." After finishing my morning prayer and meditation time, I picked up my blank pages and started writing; writing being my favorite refuge, while thoughts of butterflies and my beautiful Athena merged through my pen…

it could not have been any more

obvious, had it not flown so

purposely true, with beauty

unsurpassed; landing

with each of its teeny-tiny feet

nearly unnoticeable, if not

paying attention to new arrivals

right at the very tip-top of

my left ear, whispering

directly to me,

“all of this is just

migration.”

…wondering, what is this rapture stuff that people sometimes joke about anyway, when our pals, all around us, who we genuinely love above anyone else, are suddenly swiped-up to doggie heaven like that; I guess there’s no such thing yet as heaven’s seatbelts, trying to keep us in place while life starts jarring us all around again…

…counting on finding, one more time, that rapture of still being here, whenever feeling the-way-‘here’ arrives again… lying on the floor at purple church with my buddy AppleJacks, taking dog-naps side-by-side, surrendering to whatever’s next from our BFFFE Jesus while thinking of our beautiful Athena as she says “…don’t worry guys, take the time that you need ‘cause I gotchu…”

…with that poem still in my brain, thinking about migrating butterflies, like the whispering one that landed on the top of my ear in that poem, and how butterflies migrate for thousands of miles on their way to Mexico. It’s beautiful to see each fall, how there are suddenly butterflies everywhere, from where we live, here in their flight path. I had been curious about migrating butterflies a few years ago; wondering to myself “how can a tiny butterfly possibly fly with their tiny wings all the way from somewhere in Canada to Mexico?” And, unless what I found when I looked it up turns out to somehow be untrue, they’re able to migrate all that distance, because the migration itself is multigenerational, like a butterfly relay; the first generation getting through the first section of their path, then, the next generation getting them further, on and on and on, all across thousands of miles of the continent in a relay of butterfly generations, until the final bunch of 'em arrive in Mexico, and partaayyyyy like there's no tomorrow. Giant trees absolutely full of butterflies. It's truly incredible to see. At first, it just looks like you're seeing great big leaves up in the tops of tall trees, then, as you stop and focus for long enough, realizing, holy moly those are not just giant leaves, they're stacks and stacks of butterflies, like, literally millions of them all one right next to each other, all through all of these super tall trees.

Going back now, as you would imagine, to that small group of still rooted, bright yellow flowers, growing in the beautiful sunlight next to the empty patio chair; thinking now about migrating butterflies, having one more place to gather some flower-fuel while on their long journey. Thinking that really, all of us are just migrating from here to where's next, just like my beautiful Athena did this week; seeing that 'remaining present', instead of just wishing to be scooped-up by the next flying saucer, has some purpose left in it after all; maybe even a whole lot of purpose left. God knows better than me, so I'll just get outta the way and let Him take care of worrying about what's next and where's forward;

remembering at the same time, that "doggie heaven" is an absolutely redundant term because there's no way that there is ever gonna be
one-of-'em without the other.

Living, one more day, rooted here with purpose, right up to the time that we sing that one part of the song, where…

"…we climbed aboard their starship and headed for the sky."

…in the name of Jesus Christ, amen.

Purple Church of Jesus

♡ for everyone for forever ♡

Finding Lost Gratitude

Finding Lost Gratitude

November 27, 2025

All right, let's do it. He's a good boy; you got room over here, bud, if you want, you too, little Mar-Lee. It's dog night at Purple Church of Jesus.
Heck yeah. All right. You want to sit down? Sit down, bud. There's a good boy. There's a good boy. All right. Welcome to Purple Church of Jesus. Hey baby, welcome to Purple Church of Jesus to you too. It's your first time, huh? Got a little newcomer Mar-Lee here; wanted to check it out, so yeah.

Welcome to Purple Church of Jesus, where everyone is welcome, including our dogs. When we started Purple Church of Jesus in March of this year, I was hoping that we'd be able to have at least one gathering, at least one "not-a-sermon," and that, the "see-a-need-fill-a-need" of Purple Church of Jesus coming into existence would be seen and understood. Incredibly, to me at least, we've made it from that first time in March all the way to November; to Thanksgiving. I was hoping when we started Purple Church of Jesus that we would just be seen, and understood, and that we'd be able to have more than one of these. And incredibly, here we are, already in Thanksgiving; understood, stronger, and still here with an actual bricks and mortar space with our puppies. Thank you, God. So, as we begin tonight's not a sermon, let's --…oh, first of all, let me take my hat off. I wore this hat to remember to honor my friend Cody, who is traveling right now with his girlfriend Megan and their dogs; holiday traveling, you know, driving on these roads. And my friend Jay, also traveling with his family today; and anybody else who's traveling for these holidays, God bless you and please be

safe. So, I wanted to wear that hat to remember my brain, to honor of my friend Cody and my friend Jay and their families during their holiday travels.
Okay. So, as we begin tonight's not a sermon, let's start with a few moments of meditation as we always try to remember to do with thoughts of gratitude for everything that brought each of us here.
Just a few moments. Happy puppy dance. So great. All right, I want to start tonight with a song. That is a tradition that I have where I make an attempt at a really great song, a terrible attempt, because I have no talent (Superhero Lucas, "You always do good.") So, um, you will immediately be able to verify that what I have said is true. But I want to start this way. All right, I'm not I'm not going to try to play any crazy instrument with this. I'm just going to jump-in like our little puppy Jesús. I wonder; they may not ever calm down, and that's okay. They can have fun and play, huh, baby? Yeah. Yeah. I wonder if… well, we're good. Let's just do it. Okay.

Why me - by Kris Kristofferson

I love this song because what starts out as sounding like a song of whining about something, like "why me?", it becomes what turns out to be a song of deep gratitude, and the respect that comes with that gratitude. There's this story that I love that I've known for such a long time I can't even remember.

Oh, you're gonna eat Grover now, huh? Oh, no, no, no, no. I don't think Grover's puppy-proof. Oh boy. Nah. Oh my goodness. Grover. No. He's one of my Superheroes, but nah. Okay. Safety for Grover. Safety for Grover, please. Oh boy. Where's his little turtle? That's his turtle; he can…, this is insanity. The best kind. There you go. There's the turtle. All right, that was; that's a good one.

So, I was uh talking about this uh story from a long time ago, so long ago that I don't even remember when I heard it or where I heard it from. And, let me let me get back to here, where I was before all that greatness just happened and we got real busy saving Grover's life for a minute. Okay, this story is about a newly married couple having their first Thanksgiving together. The wife in the story is excited about preparing a great big dinner to celebrate. For the purposes of telling this story more easily, we'll have a wife-husband couple so that it doesn't get confusing for the story by saying wife-one and wife-two or husband-one and husband-two and our whole-beautiful-rainbow of alphabet letters. But it could just as easily be about any new couple having their first Thanksgiving together. So, the story goes, wife's making the Thanksgiving dinner; their first one. She's all excited. Husband's there, helping with whatever he can, watching and everything. And all of a sudden the wife, she takes the turkey, she's preparing it, and she cuts off one big chunk of it, throws it in the trash, and then finishes with all the whatever she's doing with spices and all the stuff, you know. And the husband's just like, "What? What just happened? Why'd you throw that in the trash?" She says “This is our family recipe. This is how we make a turkey in my family. It goes back generations and this is the proper way of doing it.” He's like, "Well, that's just weird that you just cut off a whole part of that turkey and threw it away and then just cook the rest." She says, "That's family recipe. Are you arguing with me? You want to talk to my mom about it?" He says, "Yeah, let's get your mom on the phone." So, they call the new wife's mom. Her mom says, "Hi, honey. Happy Thanksgiving!" The new wife says, "Happy Thanksgiving." Mom says, "How's it going for your first Thanksgiving?" new wife says, "It's going great, except for my new husband is really having a problem with our family recipe and is kind of getting a little argumentative with me, about thinking that it's silly to be chopping off a part of this turkey and tossing it out before cooking the rest; and that's our family recipe. I tried to explain to him that that's been in our family for generations and he ain't buying it. So now he's calling you to find out what's up." Mom says, "Oh, no. That's real. That's our family recipe. That's how we make a turkey for Thanksgiving, and you don't want to mess with our family's original recipe cuz this is how it's done, right?" Husband's still not buying it. He says, "What is up with this? This isn't making any kind of sense to me. Let's get grandma on the phone cuz grandma's still alive. Let's call grandma cuz I want to hear what is up with this tradition you got." They call up grandma. "Grandma, what is going on with this family recipe that we've been carrying all these years, doing every year after year after year? My new husband is being a pain about it and disagreeing with me about it. I'm just trying to make us a really nice dinner and it's kind of getting ruined by him being a stick in the mud about me doing things the way we do. So, what's up with this, grandma? Please explain to him why this is our family recipe." And grandma says, "Oh, honey, are you still doing that? Y'all still cut off part of that turkey and throw it away for Thanksgiving and you don't even cook it or eat it?" Both the mom and the new wife say, "Yeah, that's our that's our family recipe. That's our special recipe. That's the way we do it." And grandma says, "Honey," she says, "Reason I was doing that is because my pan was too small. It wouldn't all fit in there, so I had to take part of it off." Like, what?

So, it's a silly little story about how traditions can sometimes take a little bit of a wrong direction. Hi, AppleJacks! It's like, 'where… where's the turkey?' Can you lay down with me? Yeah, just just chill. You're doing so good, bud. I love you so much.

So, I wanted to start with that story. The reason that story popped into my head again after who knows how many years was through a discussion that I was having with some of my friends during a get together that we had last week. Recognizing Transgender Day of Remembrance, which in case you don't already know, happens on November the 20th of each year in remembrance of the transgender humans who were killed during that year, taking a few moments to think of each of them by name. As each of us took a turn reading their names out loud from a way-too-long list, giving some pause in-between each person's name, imagining that human being who began this year, likely without knowing that they wouldn't be here by the end of it, and reflecting on their lives. Some of them having their lives taken from them, and some of them taking their own life; connecting with them and with the life that we still have right now. During that discussion we were having as a group afterwards, we talked about how difficult it is for some families and friends, when we come out, to figure out how to manage this new family member or friend of theirs. What "box" all of this new information needs to cleanly fit into as if we, as a family member or friend, were suddenly any different from who they had already known, loved, gone through tons of stuff with and then laughed about, sometimes for multiple years. What new box does this new person standing in front of them fit into that still allows for everything great that we already had together to also fit? Do parts of our relationships need to have that connective tissue chopped off? What a way to find out about what we call 'attachment issues.' The Bible talks about leaving everybody and everything behind, if necessary, in order to follow Christ, including fathers, mothers, brothers, and sisters. And I wonder about chopping through that connective tissue, discarding what doesn't fit into that handed down heirloom casserole dish. Maybe what doesn't fit into that heirloom casserole dish is really the lesson of that scripture. Or if, through following the message of love that Jesus taught, we're given an opportunity to grow; finding a whole new Christlike casserole recipe. All of us stronger together because of following his example rather than limiting the possibilities of what truly following his example could be.

Interestingly, at least to me, the Bible also contains very clear guidance about being willing to give up all of our worldly belongings and monetary wealth to follow him. References about how difficult it is for a rich man to enter into heaven. But we don't really see very many modern examples of that same level of dedication that leads to the voluntary separation from our possessions or deep bank accounts as we routinely see, almost by default, with the sometimes-enthusiasm surrounding the separation from others who don't quite fit-in the right way. Not a squared-off human uniformly-enough to fit-in with that good home cooking. When we began Purple Church of Jesus, at the beginning of this year, the primary focus and purpose really was and is to provide a spirituality safe place and opportunity for our LGBTQIA+ community to connect with God as we are able to find, feel, honor, and celebrate our innate connection with God, either again or for the first time, free from the judgment, shame, and the exclusivity that sometimes finds itself less interested in protecting individuals, on their spiritual life journeys, if by doing that it could be perceived as being at the expense of protecting any organized religion's lock-hold on image. How many concrete boots of dogma have been used to pull spiritually-excluded souls down to the bottom of the ocean? And how many of those concrete boots have our fellow humans put on themselves, saying to themselves, "just get me out of here."

That wasted turkey leg; it's just like that. ‘What would our friends and neighbors and fellow church members say? Because this is the only dish that we've got. So, you better find a way to fit in into it or else get away.’ Easier to just eject what doesn't fit rather than having to understand or explain anything with anybody. Understanding, empathy, and God forbid; love. All front-and-center in direct combat once again, with what is culturally understood as “the way that it has always been.” If you've ever felt what involuntarily living on the wrong side of ‘the-way-it-has-always-been’ is like, you will immediately know it and you'll never forget it. You don't fit into the only dish we've got. So, you go.

There's more to this ‘throwing the baby out with a bathwater’ story; to use another analogy. As I have found, there's a whole lot more to this see-a-need-fill-a-need stewardship and mission than finding and helping the ejected sheep of our LGBTQIA+ community. There are probably literally millions of people who have become disenchanted with, or felt outright rejected by, God or Jesus Christ or their own spirituality seeking natures because of their direct experience with, or by, the examples of God's self-professed followers. In other words, there's probably a whole lot more chopped off turkey leg out there than there is turkey. To continue with that example, there's probably even a lot of that turkey that stays put inside of the perceived safety of that dish through fearfulness, keeping themselves hidden beneath that tented tinfoil because of worrying about being chopped off too. That invisible despair of being stuck in that safe-certainty of an unworthiness-whirlpool with a fake smile plastered to your face. Appearances being everything. Just don't throw me away.

The parable of the good Samaritan, that probably almost everybody's familiar with; a real famous part of the Bible, the good Samaritan. To give you some background, Samaritans and Jews; they had a deep animosity between each other. Jews didn't like Samaritans at all because Jews felt like Samaritans were "half-breeds" like they had mingled and had children with people who had moved from other places and they just didn't think that their blood was pure. Jews did not like Samaritans. So, when the parable of the good Samaritan happens; Jesus telling everybody about it, it's interesting to me that Jesus chose the Jewish person to be the one that is in the road, beaten up, dying, needing help, if you're unfamiliar with the story, and then, the Samaritan comes along. The Jew who hates Samaritans, culturally, traditionally at the time, is the one that's being rescued by a Samaritan. I wanted to read that story real quick. It's in Luke chapter 10 verses 25-37.

Hi, buddy. You want to read some Bible with me? We need to write a puppy Bible. I really want to. AppleJacks will help me, huh? Yeah. You're definitely connected with God, buddy.

So, Luke 10:25-37. And behold, a certain lawyer stood up and tested him, saying, "Teacher, what shall I do to inherit eternal life?" He said to him, He being Jesus, said to him, "What is written in the law? What is your reading of it?" So he answered and said, "You shall love the Lord your God with all your heart, with all your soul, with all your strength, and with all your mind, and your neighbor as yourself." And he, Jesus, said to him, "You have answered rightly, do this, and you will live." But, he said, wanting to justify himself said to Jesus, "And who is my neighbor?" Jesus answered and said, "A certain man went down from Jerusalem to Jericho and fell among the thieves who stripped him of his clothing, wounded him, and departed, leaving him half dead. Now by chance, a certain priest came down that road. When he saw him, he passed by on the other side. Likewise, a Levite, when he arrived at the place, came and looked and passed by on the other side. But a certain Samaritan, as he journeyed, came where he was, and when he saw him, he had compassion. So, he went to him and bandaged his wounds, pouring on oil and wine, and set him on his own animal, brought him to an inn, and took care of him. On the next day, when he departed, he took out two dinari, gave them to the inn keeper, and said to him, "Take care of him. Whatever more you spend, when I come again, I will repay you." So, which of these three do you think was neighbor to him who fell among the thieves? And he said, "He who showed mercy on him." And Jesus said to him, "Go and do likewise." The Bible, you know, I joke about it sometimes like “in Bible times,” but I mean, we are living “in Bible times” now. The Bible is still relevant now, 100%. You can easily draw parallels between what we read here and what we see every day, happening in the news today. So, I always try to bring it back to ‘what is the Bible really saying about this stuff?’ because we get so accustomed to ‘that's just the way it is,’ you know, even especially when it comes from people who are of faith, or claim faith; I always try to bring it back to, “okay, well, let's talk about the Bible sometime ‘that's the-way-it-always-is’ and your self-professed ‘Christian followers of the Bible.’ Let's talk about this a little bit more.” I think the story of the Good Samaritan is a perfect example of that.

I talk about see-a-need, feel-a-need pretty often. And the thing behind that is, one day while I was at work, I was running around; it was a busy day, super busy day. I saw a task that needed to be done. Everybody else was scurrying around; we're having a busy day and I took care of that task. It was a nothing task. It was absolutely no big deal. It was a task that needed to be done. I saw it, took care of it, and kept going. Somebody saw me do that, and he complimented me, saying, "That's awesome." He said, "See a need, fill a need. You saw that needed to happen. You just did it and kept going on your way. It was just there in front of you to do and you did it without asking or without making a big deal out of it. You just took care of it and took care of that need. See a need, fill a need." So, when I started putting together Purple Church of Jesus, it was for that reason. See a need, fill a need. The need being LGBTQIA+ humans being ejected from their churches, their families, their friendships, everything that people throw at LGBTQs and just finally getting to the point in this long life of saying, 'you know what, I just can't tolerate it. It can't be that way anymore.' The "that's-just-the-way-it-is" stops at Purple Church of Jesus. This is a totally affirming LGBTQIA+ place; the see-a-need-fill-a-need, a little bit of background. Say it over and over again. That's what I'm talking about. So, when we began Purple Church of Jesus earlier this year, it was due to the see a need fill in need of directly addressing spiritual abuse; saying what that experience is like out loud, with the mission and intention of reaching out as a true beacon on a hill to anyone and everyone who has been, or has felt like they've been, ejected, rejected, or have become spiritually lost… that impossible isolation. Left either scarred by, or actually feeling threatened by their own intrinsically individual spiritual connection with God; reminding myself of that mission. It's no wonder that Purple Church of Jesus sometimes doesn't feel like a regular church. We're building a bridge here for people who have felt like they were pushed off of a spiritual cliff, to dust ourselves off and try to find our trust in God again; just all of that. And, if possible, you ask God. I'm just here doing what God asked me to do. So yeah, if we talk about here, how it doesn't feel like a regular church to you, you're right. Purple Church of

Jesus is here for people who have felt that they'd rather burn a church down than go into one. This is our spiritual safe house where everyone is welcome; where we're safe to find and trust that bridge, either again or for the first time.

God and I are doing this together; mostly God, so you know, that's a fact.

There's a whole lot more of the story that I began this not a sermon with, going with the newlyweds and their first turkey dinner that goes beyond… it's a Wrestlemania of puppies right now, huh? This is just excitement that will not ever end. These puppies are born for church; born for Purple Church, huh? That's right. This is the best kind of place to go, puppies! The best church for puppies! Bring your puppies! Come back; or if you know somebody who wants to come to this. Always puppies are welcome. There's a water bowl, treats and everything. I need more chew toys.

Going back to our story of the turkey getting chopped and thrown away, that I began this not a sermon with, going beyond rebuilding a bridge to our connective-tissue; here it is. Think for a moment or for a few of the person or the people who never tried to get us to fit back into anyone's boxes; people who, almost like they were defying gravity, did not reject us, while it felt like everyone else around us was doing exactly that, either invisibly or right to our faces. The people who stuck around are people who would likely never think of themselves as superheroes; would laugh and immediately dismiss it if we suggested it, but it's true. The people who could see what was happening as we were being pushed off of our cliffs, and without having to know any or all of the answers to anything, continued to look us right in the eye and show us that we're seen, that we're emotionally safe with them, that we're loved no matter what, and that all of these qualities that have always connected us are a constant.

For me, this person was and is one of my big brothers, who absolutely true to form, would immediately shrug off any suggestion of approaching superhero status. But I wanted to, and had to, in the middle of this discussion about experiencing being thrown out remember those who don't, those who didn't do that, and what it feels like to honor that. Even if it means not telling that person, or a group of people about it out loud, if it makes them feel all awkward or weird about how, during that feeling of being in freefall, they reminded us, usually without even having to say any words at all, that we are still on firm ground with the lifesavers these people are; trying not to make them feel awkward by telling them that. Just respect and genuine gratitude. The point that I'm wanting to get to with that corny newlywed Thanksgiving story that I began this not a sermon with is this: Thinking about God, especially for those of us who have experienced spiritual abuse, and finding a way of letting ourselves think about God, even if it's just for a few minutes, in a non-hostile won't-fit-the-right-way in any of these boxes that I've already got, all solid-walled all around me, about God. Thinking about God for a few minutes like that, without any boxes, when nobody else is around, without necessarily even telling anyone, and without any of those automatic concrete-barriers we've got, pushing all of that comfortable old "sure-about-this" furniture up against the front door, just leaving the front door un-barricaded and unlocked, remembering the feeling of being rejected by people who would or could not let themselves even just sit there next to us, right here on firm ground, without having to understand anything about anything for a while, without fear or confusion dictating that the only options are to either completely toss out any thoughts of God ever existing, or to just hate Him right along with everyone else who's been done wrong by His followers when He becomes insistent on not leaving. And, if you're listening, you will see that, indeed, He's not leaving. In other words, not doing with our thoughts of God exactly what we've hated the most about people prejudging and condemning us before even having anything of a non-biased, non-hostile conversation.

Instead, finding that spiritual safe place, as though you're a spiritual-run-away; away from everybody and everything cuz none of our understanding or relationship with God was ever up to any of them to decide for any of us anyway, no matter how much they would like for it to be, saying "hey God what's up, besides You, hah - that is corny I know, but you'll get used to that, God, because and in fact, thanks in advance for every corny joke that I will ever tell you because there are a lot and I like to laugh about stuff. Anyway, that's it for now God; saying hi for a second without everyone else throwing rocks at us both because this is just about You and me; period."

There's a poem somewhere, if I can find it. You know what is it in the book? Yeah, I think there's some right next to you over there. (Superhero Lucas) "I was going to say I have your book in my car." Cool. I got a few of them right over there. Just down on the near the floor maybe. No; did I put them up there, underneath stuff? Yeah, just a second. Yeah, cool. Thanks. Appreciate it. Let's see what I find; hello, buddy. I'll find it. I think this is it. Yep.

This one's called spring forward, fall back. about how people prejudge and then immediately reject people from the LGBTQ community the same way we sometimes do the same thing about thoughts of God, and with thinking about God because of that spiritual trauma; the spiritual abuse that just gets into our PTSD of "why would I go near that?

I'd rather light that church on fire than approach thoughts about God.” So, trying to suspend that, just for a moment, as we would hope people would suspend judgment of us in the LGBTQ community; this is that poem, called spring forward and fall back:

You may still
hate me
and people who like and who are like me,
but you will
no longer be able to
so easily
or so automatically
have your hate spill over
what you have given yourself
the slightest permission
to see.

Just give it a minute to look without judgment, even without anybody around you, to say, "How do I really feel?". Just lay that “sure-about-this” prejudgment down. Crack jokes with God. It's fun.

Traditionally, at every Thanksgiving, giving a minute or two of pause for some gratitude before gorging ourselves on that third piece of pie is all that's required. And even that level of gratitude could probably just be phoned in. But, here's the thought that I wanted to bring for our Thanksgiving not-a-sermon today. Thinking this time, what about what we've already tossed-out through fear or confusion or generationally taught hostility? Chopping off that part, throwing it away, because it don't fit-in-the-dish. Finding, within each of us, that one possibility that perhaps something, or someone we couldn't quite make fit the right way, has some undiscovered characteristic or outright-dismissed-element that's worthy of our gratitude, that has been right here all along, just waiting for us to pull the "sure-of-this" couch barricades away from the door and saying "hey, I've just got a minute, what's up?" trying to not have that same automatic knee-jerk reaction to thoughts about God, that those of us from the LGBTQIA+ community all know all-too-well, and have all felt from so many others all through life, who would rather automatically attack or dismiss than to just sit down for a five minute conversation, to find our firm ground again with God. That, my beautiful friends and puppies everywhere is where you'll find the respect that comes with gratitude. Worth finding your voice for, even if it's just to say thank you;

a lifetime source of strength and love, worthy of trust at a level that cannot be interfered with by anybody.

A song that came on the stereo when I was driving around the other day. I was listening to it, and I'm getting goosebumps again just thinking about it right now because it was just so great. And man, before I knew it, it was like a Christian song, you know, and I just was listening to it and singing it. I was singing as best I could because I didn't know it, but just, you know, going along with it. By the time that I was just driving through the hills out here in the Hill Country, in the dark, in the middle of nowhere, hearing that song for the first time, it was just like I was just shouting it out. I was it was like I was at a Van Halen concert or something because it was just so moving and so beautiful and so great and I really felt it and hi buddy, I love you AppleJacks. So, I'm going to give it a try. It ain't going to be good, but I'm going to give it a try because this song really did it for me. I'll be quick and, if it's terrible I promise I'll stop; which it will be, you have that guarantee already built-in.

I'm going to try, which is really all of this, you know. I mean, when I when I showed up and started Purple Church of Jesus, I saw the see a need fill a need. I didn't know what the heck I was doing. I just asked God, what do you want me to do? And this came to me as direction from God. And I was like… I don't know how you mean for me to start a church. Are you serious with this, God? Start a church in a little town of Texas; being all LGBTQIA affirming AF? This big gay church where you go if you're gay and you've been rejected, ejected, hated, spiritually abused; gosh, that's just so terrible when that happens. When people say 'you don't deserve to be near God, God judges you, hates you, you need to change everything about you or at least act like you're not who you are in order for you to have the ability to love and worship and feel strength from God and God's people.' That's just so wrong. There has got to be a place that will help people to know that that's a whole bunch of horseshit all buzzing with flies and everything. Believe it.

You belong here, and you can find God exactly as-you-are and because-of-who-you-are, not "in spite of who you are." You are loved; exactly who you are. What you bring to the world, exactly who you are, is exactly what the world needs. You find that with the strength from God, the direction from God, and holy moly; you're ready. When that came to me and I was asking God, are you serious? I didn't know what I was doing. I just showed up and said, "Show me God. I don't know what I'm doing." So that's where I am. I say that long story because I ain't no "new-church-maker." That's obvious to anybody who's paid any attention. And I ain't no singer, but you know, I hear something, and it moves me, I want to share it and I'm going to do the best I can with what I got. Just like my mom taught me.

Let me try something. That's all right, AppleJacks. We can still stay in here for now. Let's see if this will play. There it is. [music] All right. Now it's the calm time, baby. And then we're done. Okay. Then we can play. All right. We're going to try this. You want to sit down with me? See if I can follow along best I can with what I got. Ready? Just wanted to show no matter what, I was excommunicated from my church when I was 21. People felt like I was not worthy. So, singing this song just to help people see that it don't matter what anybody says. Your relationship with God is your relationship with God. Nobody gets to get in. Nobody gets to get in the middle of that. Nobody. Don't let him ever. All right, [music] [clears throat] here we go, bud. We're gonna try.

Gratitude - by Brandon Lake

I hope and I pray we can all find the spiritual strength that is right there in front of us; that we don't let anybody shame us away from finding that, feeling that, loving that, living that, breathing that, having that be every part of our lives every day. Anybody that tries to get in the way of that, interfere with that… in a nice way, tell them that they can just uh depart -hah- because nobody's interfering with that. Once you feel that, once you know that, once you found that, once it's there with you; start a new day with it. There's a lot of people who think that they've got to cut off part of that turkey. That don't make it true. <u>My point of directly addressing spiritual abuse</u> is to hopefully help build that bridge for people who have felt like there's no way that they would want to have anything to do with God again, based on how they felt from people who profess to believe in God; the abuse that they experienced in their homes, their communities, and at churches. Find that safe place here. Find that safe place wherever you are. Feel it. Breathe it. Live it. And don't let anybody take that from you no matter what. That's it. I say all these things, and I am so grateful that y'all are here; our puppies too, they have been feeling the spirit the whole time. I say this in the name of Jesus Christ. Amen. Amen.

Purple Church of Jesus

♡ for everyone for forever ♡

He Found Me
December 10, 2025

Alright, good morning. I'm just going to talk real quickly here about stuff that I want to remember to put in my not-a-sermon this week. So, as I fasten my seat belt, the 99 and the one, like, the sheep that Jesus found. Hold on. Click. There we go. Yeah, it was like that. Jesus found me; click. All right. So, I don't know if this is recording. I'm going to really try to hope… well, I am hoping that it's recording, but I'm going to really try to convey my thoughts while I'm driving. Just quickly note that uh, Jesus finding the lost sheep, you know, I got this t-shirt, purple t-shirt, like a football jersey that says "He left the 99 to find the one" find me, you know, and that is absolutely true. To feel that, and… to really feel that; it's like, He found me, you know, and… oops, I think that I just put my car in neutral. Let me stop and put myself back in drive cuz I'm just not used to how to make this thing work yet. Okay, here we go. Think. All right, stuff is on. Yeah it is. Okay, so yeah, He found me. I mean, He Found Me! And He's filling me with light like I'm a little jack-o-lantern here just beaming and I mean I absolutely feel that and it is all the way true and it is all the way just full of shining light inside of me. There's just no way to contain it. It just is. I mean, I just feel like I'm flying still. And today is the 10th, so it's 4 days since I've been baptized; 4 days since I praised Jesus, you know, said His name, and I love You and I follow You and You are my Savior and Thank You for the Grace. Thank You for the price that You paid. Thank You for my salvation. I honor You and I thank You and I praise You and You Found Me, you know. And, thinking about the 99 and the one, feeling like that one, you know, it's like there's one thing for Jesus to find you, because he does. But then, there's a whole 'nother thing about knowing you're found. I mean, it isn't just like you're moving along and all-of-a-sudden your life changes; like, changes-changes, cuz that happens to people, you know. But, I mean, feeling like He found me. He got me. He Found Me. I don't know how He found me. I mean, of course He found me. He's Jesus. That's what He does. That's what He does. He finds you. He saves you. He's with you. And He keeps you with him. You know, I mean, I just can't, I don't know how to convey that most clearly other than just Praise God! Praise God! I'm found! Jesus found me and I feel it and I know it and I'm found! Praise God! Praise God! You know, and I was thinking about the other 99. I'm like, "okay, well, but He left the 99 to find one. He left the 99 to find me." You know, I'm no better than anybody else. Why. Why would he leave 99 that are just as important as me, that he loves just as much as me, which is <u>a lot</u>, <u>a lot</u>. I hope that you feel how that <u>'a lot'</u> feels sometime; if you haven't yet. I just hope you do. But, He left 99 to find me and I'm not more important than those 99. So, how can He just do that, you know? I thought how, when we are saved, when we know that we've got God with us, when we have Jesus in our hearts, living inside of us, and us inside of Him and we are one, it's like, He's still with those 99. He can go look for that one and He does go look for them and He finds them. But that doesn't mean that the 99 did not have Him with them the entire time that He was going and getting that one, however He does, because oh my goodness, I was so lost. How in the world did He find me? And, <u>of course</u> He found me, at the same time, and how-in-the-world-on top-of-all-of-that am I able <u>to feel and know the truth of I've been found</u>. All of that is amazing to me. All of that is a miracle to me. But He did not just leave the 99 to wander and wonder and be lost so He could find me. No. They had Him already. They have Him. He's kept them and they've kept Him. He is in their hearts. He lives in them like He lives in me. So yeah, this is all real stuff. Find Him. Let Him find you. Feel what that feels like to feel found. I pray to God that you do. I love you. I love you, Jesus. Thank you for what you have done with me and what we continue to do together. And thank you for reassuring me and letting me know that those 99, you love them just like you do me, and they got you with them just like you are with me. I love you, God. Praise God! Thank you, God. In your holy name, Jesus Christ, I love you, amen.

Purple Church of Jesus
greatness
greatness
be what is
for everyone for forever

Praise God!
Praise God!
December 11, 2025

All right, here we go, babies. You want to have a seat back here with me, little Mar-Lee? Here we go. Got a little spot right here for you. You too, AppleJacks. All right, let's have us some Purple Church of Jesus. Okay, right. Let me adjust this cushion. You can sit down. It's ok, bud. All right, my good babies. Oh, look at this. I got a little what's that? A puppy treat with th letter "B" for beautiful; "B" for beautiful. Yeah, you want one? You can keep one more for after, one for after church. Okay. Come on over here, Mar-Lee. Can you come over here? And we've got room here for you too, AppleJacks. That's it. There's my pups. Okay, come have a seat, bud.

Welcome to Purple Church of Jesus, where everybody's welcome and everybody's beautiful, huh? Yeah, that's' right. That's right. I see you. Thank you for being here with me, the beautiful puppies of Purple Church of Jesus. You know, I really had a wonderful time with our open mic, earlier tonight, and thank God. Praise God for every bit of conversation we're able to have around how we find our spiritual path; stay true to our spiritual path, truly, because we're on a spiritual path. We can get lost, but our compass will keep on working. You know, I was raised Mormon; oops, Latter Day Saints. We used to call ourselves Mormons, but that's changed now. Church of Jesus Christ of Latter Day Saints, and reading the Book of Mormon and the Bible, to help dispel any myth or rumor about the Morm… The Church of Jesus Christ of Latter Day Saints; people saying that they don't follow the Bible. Yes, they do; 100% they do. They believe that God is who we're getting our way back to and Jesus Christ is his Son on earth, the Son of God. He paid for our sins and it is through Jesus Christ that we can have redemption and salvation; that He paid the price for our sins, the ultimate price, in the Garden of Gethsemane; He hung on the cross for our sins. He is our big brother. He is our guide. That's how I was raised to believe as a Latter Day Saint. A lot of people don't really pay a lot of attention to, or understand much about the Church of Jesus Christ of Latter Day Saints. And, like with a lot of things, once it's judged to be a certain thing, whether or not it's misunderstood, it's not looked into any further; I'm not here to have a Purple Church of Jesus about the Church of Jesus Christ of Latter Day Saints tonight, but that's my path. That's where I came through; the Church of Jesus Christ of Latter Day Saints. And you know, I've gone through several layers of finding my path after being excommunicated from that church for being gay. A lot has changed since then, but not enough so that I could just say, "Hey, it's only this church or only that church." So that's why we have this church. Purple Church of Jesus, where you are all welcome, along with all the pups.

No church is going to have any power over you. You find God. God's the one. God has got you. No matter what any other church, who doesn't want you says; let's find that. In that conversation, and within that wing of the conversation with Purple Church of Jesus, relating back to the Church of Jesus Christ of Latter Day Saints, or to say LDS, in the Book of Mormon, which accompanies the Holy Bible as another testament of Jesus Christ, fully the same way of scripture. There's a group of people called Nephites who were traveling across the ocean to come to the new world, and, they followed a God-given compass called the Liahona. This is how they found their way across uncharted waters, from the old world to the new world, without even knowing for sure where they were going, which is really kind of an amazing thing that a lot of us get a chance to do some version of during our lives. In the Purple Church of Jesus, that's how we find God. Just follow that Liahona that we've all got. Listen to God speaking through your intrinsically spiritual nature; being true to that instead of getting pulled this way and that way. The father of lies is very cunning and deceptive and has a number-one goal of getting us disconnected from God. If you stay true to your intrinsically spiritual being, call it the Liahona if you want, or call it Julie Andrews, for me. Not the real Julie Andrews; a suspension of disbelief that comes with a feeling of 'God doesn't hate me and I don't hate God.' Whether or not I need to put Julie Andrews' face on that feeling for a while, so that I don't feel the abusive feeling towards God that I grew up with towards gay people; me being pitted against me, like those old Mad Magazine "Spy vs. Spy" comic strips.

God became Julie Andrews. I can see God through Julie Andrews, twirling and being happy and not hating me and me not hating her, or Him. And yes, the thought of that is just me saying "follow your spiritual path and it'll get you there." Might be like, with me, wandering through the desert for 40 years, like Moses. Literally, 41 years from the time that I got excommunicated I've been saved. This week, I was re-baptized. My feelings had been 'if they raised me to believe what is bound on earth is bound in heaven, and what was loosed on earth is loosed in heaven when I was excommunicated at 21…' I was like, 'I'm just going to cross those Ts.' "Cross-T"… wow, that just happened. That was really cool. Thank you, Jesus! Praise God! Thank you, Jesus. Wow. Jesus crossed that T for me today, or this week. Cross those Ts and dot those eyes.

You might think that I was loosed in heaven, me being excommunicated meant maybe or maybe not my baptism

was also non-existent anymore. I thought, you know, I should be re-baptized, which happened this week on Saturday, whatever the 6th was, and literally transformed like… beam of light transformed; like… I hadn't seen that coming transformed. And that's just like 'that was not on my bingo card, what just happened this week.'
That came from, you can call it "Liahona" or whatever you want to call it. Being true to your spiritual-core-nature. Even if people on this one side are saying "No, you're full of it because of blah blah blah." People on that other side saying "No, you're full of it because of blah blah blah." Everybody wants to quack at you all the way, you know.

Going in our open mic part tonight, I was talking about imagining being in a big stadium; oh, my AppleJacks you are such a good boy. Full of people who all have an opinion and all want to throw rocks at you if you don't follow what they say with their opinions. And just being able to walk straight across a football field, or 100 football fields with that noise on both sides. If you keep your eye on God, on that spiritual path that God's got you on, it doesn't matter if it takes a week, a day, a minute, or 41 years. You keep your eye on that. You can call it "Liahona." You can call it "Julie Andrews doesn't hate me so I can have a relationship with God again after going through spiritual abuse rather than throwing all of it out and saying 'because they said that, then I must not have any relationship with God', so I might as well just toss it all out." Keep your eye on that light. Keep your eye on that beam.

That's what I wanted to talk about tonight; briefly. We'll keep it quick because there's… this is the rest of life now. I'm serious. You know, in the LGBTQ+ community, transgender humans who don't identify with the gender they were identified as being, at birth, go through a period of transition, transformation, as they are able to hone-in on their identity, who they are, who they feel they are. Of course they get people judging them, and hating them, and everything like that. But they go through a transformation of an amazing finding-of-themselves.

I feel the same way about what happened this weekend. I got baptized and was given the gift of the Holy Spirit; Saved. Praise God! I'm going to tell you something that you just, you just… God, I'm going to meditate on this a second. I went through a Bible study with a group for 12 weeks; each week, fantastic. Each week, I would leave that Bible study just feeling so close to God and so, just full of the Spirit of God. And I was so grateful every time that I went, every week, and being told that we'd be having a two-day full-on thing at the end of this twelve weeks, and it was going to be like 90% of the whole thing, compared to what we had just been over for the previous weeks. And I thought, how is that possible? But this… what just happened to me this past weekend, I'll tell you this: We were a group of people praying over each other and I was just like, God… I'm… You just… I know that You've got me. I'm just going to follow You, and You show me what You want me to do. On the open mic part of tonight, I compared that to when I met my wife, this fantastic, loving, beautiful, full-of-light human being that I thank God I met and we fell in love with each other. But, the way I knew that it was true with the two of us was that when I moved forward with her, and the trust and the love and the joy, it just kept growing, growing, growing, it felt more solid, more true, instead of my previous existence with every… not everything in life, but a lot. It's like, it's going to fall out; the bottom is going to fall out. What brings me joy is doomed. And so, moving forward with her and our love with each other, led to our getting married. Happiest day of my life; still. But, guess what? I've got three happiest days of my life now. The day I became a missionary, when I was

19, the day that I married my wife, and the day that I was Saved. I'm 62, almost 63 years old. I have three days where, those days are like; that's what holds me up. In every one of those days, I was being true to my nature. Every one of those I was following God. Every one of those filled me with light that will never go away. I had those experiences with meeting and marrying my wife, but with this Bible study that I was doing with my friends, and every step I'd be like "well, I don't know" move forward in faith, feels good, feels true, feels right, feel the light, feel the purpose, feel the power, feel the direction, all those things, move another step forward. My poem, that I talk about 'the blind shall see' is exactly that; you move forward, you feel all of that strength, that nourishment, and if you are somebody who has had spiritual abuse, even with that, you go and you get all that validation, verification from God, "this is true, this is your path" you're still like "well… maybe." Move forward another bit, in your spirit, in your heart, and your trust of God, the One, not all these people that want to quack over here or these people that want to quack over there or down there. Lots of quacking. Go this way, that way, you know… sparkly object sparkly object. You watch God; move forward to God, in faith, in trust, knowing that is the One you can trust, that's got you… it gets bigger, go forward… bigger still… Well, if you've got spiritual abuse in your heart, in your head, that was planted there by people who pulled you away from God and into their own dogma, or their own ego, or their own fear-control foundational base of 'we're the only right ones; if you don't do it our way, then...' you're doomed, or an atheist, or not with God. Quack quack quacky quack quack. Follow God. You will find where that Liahona is trying to guide you. Find that in you. Keep moving forward like that. After a while, you don't even have to ask questions. I don't have to say why or where or how or when. Just tell me what you want me to do, God. That's what I will do. I give my life to You. You are who I trust. That is the transformation of your spirit, of your soul. I never anticipated this; feeling like this. And here, we move forward. So, thank God. Praise God. You feel that?

I wanted to read a quick story from the Bible in the book of Acts. My puppies are like, "Hey pops, we did the open mic. Isn't it time to go home? Cuz there's uh, stuff to do at home." Yeah, we'll go home in a little bit. We've just got to do a little bit of this; what I wanted to bring forward about this week. So, a chaplain friend of mine and I were talking this week, and we did that thing where… I don't know if you've ever done it, where you just open the Bible to whatever page, just a random page. We had a Bible and we're like, hey let's just open this to wherever. So, we did, and, this is what we found. this is what we opened right to. It's a little bit of a read but it's worth it because the backstory really tells the story of where it went. So, this is in Acts chapter 12, and I'll read the whole thing. If you want to grab your Bible you can read it with me. Or, if you want to read it later, just remember Acts chapter 12, like, 12 apostles. Acts… act in faith… 12 apostles. There you go. See, how I think in my brain like every second Thursday, every second matters. Acts chapter 12, action for God, 12 apostles. There you go. Now maybe you'll remember it and we're going to read the first part of it with Acts. Here we go.

Now, about that time, this is starting with Herod. About that time, Herod the king stretched out his hand to harass some of the church. Imagine that. You threaten power, guess what's going to happen? They're going to come for you, man. You've got to stay with your eyes on God. They come at you, throwing those rocks or coming at you with a king who wants to kill you. What do you do? Look to God. It doesn't matter what happens on either side of that. You follow God. God's got you. Trust God. Find a place of trusting God. You will never forget that and you will know that's where to go. So anyway, Herod's trying to pull them off to the side; sparkly object, threat there, fear here, ego there, control here. You know, all the tricks of the devil, for real. You've got to know this is the closer your tractor beam is on God, the more there's going to be pew! pew! pew! Is that the right word? It's like you're in an asteroid game. Okay. Acts 12. Remember that. "Now, about that time, Herod the king stretched out his hand to harass some from the church. Then he killed James." That's how this chapter starts. James has just been killed. James. Then he killed James, the brother of John, with a sword. Acts 12. And because he saw that it pleased the Jews, he proceeded further to seize Peter also. He's like, "Hey, I got everybody doing rah-rah-rah. Must be doing something right. I'm going to go get another one." There you go. Peter on his way to jail. So, he proceeded further to seize Peter also. Now it was during the days of unleavened bread. So when he had arrested him, he put him in prison and delivered him to four squads of soldiers to keep him, intending to bring him before the people after Passover because he's going to do it again. He just got James killed by a sword. James. Our James, brother of John, starts it by swording him to death. Now he's going after Peter because it's making the crowds all happy. Imagine that. Not a surprise at all. Remember "Bible times?" Yeah. Living it, people. Okay, so when he had arrested him, he put him in prison and delivered him to four squads of soldiers to keep him, intending to bring him before the people after Passover for a big spectacle, big show. Rah-rah-rah. Rah-rah-rah. Peter was therefore kept in prison, but constant prayer was offered to God for him by the church. And when Herod was about to bring him out, that night Peter was sleeping, bound with two chains between two soldiers, and the guards before the door were keeping the prison. Now behold, an angel of the Lord stood by him, and a light shone in the prison, and he struck Peter on the side, and raised him up, saying, "Arise quickly." And his chains fell off his hands. Then, the angel said to him, "Gird yourself, and tie on your sandals." And so he did. And he said to him, "Put on your garment and follow me." So when he went out and followed him, and did not know that what was done by the angel was real, but thought he was seeing a vision. When they were past the first and second guard posts, they came to the iron gate that leads to the city, which opened to them of its own accord and they went out and went down one street. And immediately the angel departed from him. And when Peter had come to himself and he said, "Now I know for certain that the Lord has sent his angel and has delivered me from the hand of Herod and from all of the expectation of the Jewish people." So when he had considered this, he came to the house of Mary, the mother of John, whose surname was Mark, where many were gathered together praying. James has just been killed by a sword; wasn't **the** sword, that's the Word of God. I guarantee you that it's a sword of the enemy. Armor of God. You know about the Armor of God. It wasn't the Word of God that was the sword that killed James. I guarantee you that. But the devil will make something look like, "Oh, this must be the way." There you go. Off to that sparkly object. Look at that light coming right at you. Follow God. You're going to be pulled off to the side by some sparkly object. Next thing you know, you're part of a group that's shoving a sword through James.

Be aware of who you listen to. Follow that beam. You're going to have quacking on both sides. Follow that beam. Peter had come to himself now. I know for certain that the Lord has sent his angel and has delivered me from the hand of Herod and from all the expectations of the Jewish people. So, when he had considered this, he came to the house of Mary, the mother of John, whose surname was Mark, for many were gathered together praying. And as Peter knocked at the door of the gate, a girl named Rhoda came to answer. When she recognized Peter's voice, she did not open the gate. This is… I love this part. She was so happy she didn't even open the gate, but she ran and announced that Peter stood before the gate. She was just overcome with joy and excitement that Peter's there. She didn't even... she just went "Ah!" and took off, so happy; didn't even think about opening the gate. She's like "I got to tell everybody Peter's here." So, she goes in her gladness. She did not open the gate, but ran in and announced that Peter stood before the gate. But they said to her, "you are beside yourself." I mean, who listens to kids? Kids have so much truth. They're telling Rhoda "You are beside yourself" as she kept insisting that it was so. So, they said, "It is his angel." Now, Peter continued knocking. And when they opened the door and saw him, they were astonished, maybe saying "Hey, we should have listened to Rhoda" and Rho is like, "See??"

Motioning to them with his hand to keep silent, he declared to them how the Lord had brought him out of prison. And he said, "Go tell these things to James and the brethren." And he departed and went to another place. Acts 12. Be in action; 12 apostles. Acts 12. That's how I'll remember it. But, the interesting part, one of them, is when he's still in prison. Angel shows up. James has just been killed. You know, there's bloodthirst in the crowd. Herod can't wait to do the same thing to Peter because he's loving all that adoration by feeding the bloodthirst of the crowd out there demanding more, more get 'em, get 'em… in "Bible times." Guess what kind of times we're in now? "Bible times." So, that's all happening; angel shows up to get Peter. Chains fall off. Angel says, "Get your shoes on. Get your clothes on. Get your cloak on. Come with me." Peter doesn't know what's going on. He just moves forward. He's got that faith. He's looking at that beam. He knows 'I don't have to have all the answers. I just know that this is the thing that I need to do right now.' Well, you know, the guards are all sleeping or there's something that's happened that's made them not aware of the situation or something. There goes Peter. Put on his clothes and his cloak like he was told, his shoes like he was told, saying "Why? I'm in prison, but yeah, I'll do what you say." And there they go, when otherwise, Herod would have killed him the next day. Showing up to see his friends, and this point of excitement at seeing him, is not even believed by anybody in the house because his fate had been met already the day before, when he was put in prison. So how could that possibly be true?

I say this because of how amazing, to be talking with a chaplain friend of mine at work, and us just having a beautiful, random conversation, and her saying "Hey, let's open the Bible and see what's there." I went straight to Rhoda, because I'm thinking of that television show in the 70s. Like… there's a Rhoda in the Bible? I thought that was a TV show name. Let's read about Rhoda. So, we're reading about Rhoda getting excited and running off to get her family and them not believing her. And then, the chaplain that I was talking with, awesome person, Theresa, I love you. She says, "Well, look, the interesting thing is right before that. Peter is totally acting in faith. He's just saying 'Oh, you want me to put on my shoes?' He's not saying 'Well, why? Let's talk about this. What's next? What's going on? Who are you? How did you get in here? Why is there all of a sudden this change, where, you know, I'm just sitting here in prison, locked up, and now you're telling me to put on my shoes. Why would I even need to do that?'" Not wasting any time. Well, cloak too. 'What… is it cold outside? Is it raining? Why do I need that? I'm not even going anywhere anyway, and you know, my cloak is kind of tucked under that sleeping guard there a little bit and what if I wake him up when I pull it out from under him?' No questions. He's just like a beam. He's on a beam. He knows. He trusts God, and he has developed his faith and the strength and belief and had that transformation that I just talked about with God. He just knows. He's like, "Yep. Okay, here we go." Cloak, shoes, chains fell off, doors open. Out they go. Past all the guards. Gates open. Get to his friends' place where they were certain he would have been doomed already or at least locked up forever. So surprised that they don't even believe that he's there. And there he is. And he is in such a, I mean, he's in such a state of just follow God, he doesn't even know what's going on to the point of it's true, that this is him talking about the same James that was just killed a little bit ago, he doesn't even know. He just knew to follow God. Follow that light. Follow that being.

You know, what we're doing here with Purple Church of Jesus is nowhere near any of this epic amazing stuff that you can open to any random page in the Bible, and all of a sudden you're reading a story of inspiration like that, of just amazement like that. But, just like the bad stuff happens, like when you say "oh, in Bible times" I mean these kinds of things are happening now. I didn't have an angel show up before Purple Church even began, and say "Hey, why don't you start a Purple Church of Jesus, Todd, because, the spiritual abuse you're seeing all around you, and that you've experience in this 41-year wander through the desert isn't going away. In fact, it's getting worse and we need your help." God is saying "Do that thing." Me, going "Wow, how about I just put on my shoes then, God. How about I find my cloak and try to do that without waking up that guard that would probably rather throw his sword through me, too;" and, it wouldn't matter if he did, because I'm following God. I'm doing what God said to do.

That's kind of how Purple Church of Jesus began. Not on an epic level, but we are in "Bible times."

You, find that Liahona. Find your spiritual path. Find what is true to your core. It doesn't matter who is quacking on either side of it. You just know and you go. The rest will figure themselves out because they're on their own journeys too. You show yourself to God and say, "God, I love you. I follow you. Praise God. I'm here. You're the One." God trusts me back, saying "Okay, here's the thing. Put on your shoes. Get your cloak. You've got places to go." I'm like, "I don't know where we're going. I don't know where this is going. I don't know what you want me to do, but I trust you more than anybody; the only One, ultimately." Here we go. Gates opening. Guards not even paying attention, or asleep, or in a daze, or who knows what, until I get to a point where there's Rhoda at the gate, going "What? How are you here, Peter?" Me feeling like, "What? How is all of this happening to me; with me?" It's not about me. It's God happening through me to the point where I get Saved this past weekend. And, I'll tell you this, people were praying over me. Forty years… forty-one years, well, more than that because it was before I'd even been excommunicated. All the shame, all the abandonment, the disgust thrown at me. It was like a vision. It was. It was like I had this visual while I was being prayed over before my baptism. I broke down. I just broke down. I just started sobbing. There was one of our friends there, that was praying over me, and I was just, I don't think I've ever been that overwhelmed with the Spirit except for when I was actually re-baptized and saved. This person who was praying over me, who didn't even know me, barely knew my name other than me walking up and "oh, hey Todd." Hi. Next thing, he's praying over me. I could feel the sense of healing that I would have never seen coming; the healing that happens in the Bible, like Jesus healing the leper.

Here's this person who has been outcast from all of society, who is covered with disease, who everybody is afraid of. Everybody is "Ah, if you get near me that's going to get on me too." You're banished. Go to your own island. Yeah, we don't have room for you here, Mister Leper. And he's, meanwhile, just covered with lesions, dying, his body being eaten alive by the disease that is crawling all over his body. And while I was in that moment, with that human who I had never met before, who knew nothing about me, praying over me, there was a sense of healing that I can't even describe. Praise God! Praise God! Oh, my… Praise God! Thank you, God! It was like all of the shame, all of the judgment, all of the hatred, all of the ugliness that had been thrown at me, all of the rejection, all of the 'you don't… you can't be here… you're not one of the righteous ones… you're not right with God… you're way over there… get on that island, leper.' It was while that human was praying with me, praying over me, it was like I visualized it, I could see it, like my spirit was covered with lesions like leprosy, all up my legs. I can still see it in my mind, how I could see it at that moment, like my legs and all of my body just lesions, on my spirit; like leprosy. That human was praying over me, praying with me, didn't know me but praying right through God coming through this human. I could see this, with my eyes closed, and me in that moment feeling the power of God come through that human to me. It was like those lesions were falling off of my spirit. I'm serious. I could see it. I could see all of it. You know what… I've been sounding like this ever since I was saved. You talk about transformation. You know it if you've experienced it. You'd never be able to deny it. If you've experienced what I've just experienced, that is the truth. Change happened. It was miraculous. Change happened that I would have never… It's like 'have faith. Yeah. Follow God. Read the Bible. Do the right thing. Be nice to your neighbor.' All of that is true and good and great and that's part of the path.

But to be transformed, to feel the Spirit of God move through you, change you, save you, transform you; Praise God!

If you haven't felt that, moving toward 'Okay, I can trust it. I'll go a little bit further. Okay, move forward. I can trust it still. Move it a little bit further. The floor isn't falling out yet. None of this stuff that feels like no-this-is-just-quacking from either side or below. I can trust this. It's growing. It's the strength, the beauty, the power, the truth, the love, the purpose. All of those things grow every time I keep moving toward that light. I'm going to trust it another step. I'm going to trust that this bottom ain't going to fall out because this feels right.' Move another step forward. Boom. It's bigger, like, this keeps on validating exactly the direction I'm going in and I'm going to move another step in faith, forward. Boom; like, what's happening right now? I've been like this for a week now. It won't, I don't think it'll ever stop. I think this is now. This is… I've been…it's a transformation. Anybody that talks to you about it, that has experienced it, believe them. You'll know by listening to them if they're full-of-it or if they're quacking from this or that or saying 'you have to do it my way' or whatever. You follow that beam. You'll know because that beam will say "Hey, yeah, I'm glad you're looking this way now. I love you, too. I trust you, too. Let's keep going." And you find a transformation happening within you that you cannot deny. That is what happened with me; as that human was praying with me, I was, honestly I mean, you live for the length of time that I've lived and have people throwing judgment, hatred, shame, fear, wanting to control you, pull you back this way, that way, fit their design, messing your brain up, your spirit up, the whole time for 40 years since the time I was excommunicated; this was since I was a teenager. I'm like, "Oh my gosh, I'm going to be in trouble with God" all my life because with everybody that I believed in, telling me that... If you don't know of it being a thing, maybe it's something to pray about so you can find out.

There's a whole lot of spiritual abuse thrown around; it doesn't have to just be at LGBTQ+ humans. Anybody that doesn't fit your dogma; Pharisees are doing it all the time. 'No! And, uh, this period is over here, and the comma is over there, and then, so that means that this word meant that and that word meant this and so that means you're not doing it the right way and if you don't do it the right way we're going to have to kill you, or you deserve to be killed.' Pharisees, doing that all the time. They totally miss the point of Jesus, you know.

That is happening in the real world, where you can go marching down the middle of that football field, or twenty of them, stadiums full, and all are going to be 'but that period was there when that comma was there; I don't know whether that needed to be a capital letter or a small letter but you did it wrong so you don't deserve to live...' from both sides. You keep your eye on that beam. You'll know because God will tell you "I got you. Stay in that tractor beam. I got you." You come through something that ended with, didn't end, began really, with me this weekend, continuing in that journey like I said; kept going bam bam bam and then, next thing I know, somebody's praying over me who doesn't even know me and feeling that channel through that human, the Spirit of God healing my spirit to the point where I can see in my mind, with my eyes closed, lesions that had been climbing all the way up my soul that I didn't even know were there, that I didn't know how to put words for, and seeing those fall off one by one by one by one, like they were scales falling off of me, healing the leper. You think that was in Bible times? They had lepers. They had to live on an island in Bible times. Look at what happens to our LGBTQ+ community today. Every day. Every day. Worse and worse and worse; just stadiums of people that can't wait to throw their dogma rocks at that human being, or at that LGBTQIA+ human being believing in God. People who have been spiritually abused by the people on the other side of the stadium, saying "You're believing in God? That's a bunch of hogwash" and throwing their rocks from that side, too. You walk through the middle of that, with both of them sure that they're the-right-ones… they're the-right-ones… they're the-right-ones. You know what? Theres One. You find that One being, you follow that light; you will be transformed. I praise God. I praise God. There's… there's… I praise God.

I don't know how He brought me this far. I don't know how He kept His eyes on me… through each other. God works through all of us. If we're true to God, guess what? God ain't just like "Okay, there you go. There's your easy chair. Glad I found you, glad you found me. Have a seat. Nice, comfy seat there. Here's, you know, a nice big sippy-soda. You can have that and relax. You made it." No. That light of God, that was shining through that human who helped me to heal from stuff that I didn't even know I could heal from, ever; those scales were falling off of my spirit. I promise you that is exactly how it felt. That is exactly what I could actually see in my mind with my eyes closed. An image that I had never thought of before. I had never thought of my spirit being covered by lesions of leprosy. Never until that moment, when I could see them all over my spirit, falling off like scales one at a time as that human prayed over me and I sobbed and sobbed and there were no words for what I was experiencing. That "Praise God!" is like the holy version of "Supercalifragilisticexpialidotious." He's just… Praise God! There's nothing you can say when you feel that way but "Praise God! Praise God!" I didn't know this was going to be happening to me.

Transformation that is possible like that, for a human like me. Praise God. Praise God. That light that shined through that human being to me, to help me feel that healing experience, to be re-baptized right after that… there's no such thing as time… all as one. All of this experience is like it's own planet-universe.

I have got to remember to slow down. This is how I am. This is how I get. This is how everybody who has seen me over this past week, who has known me for a long time, says "What has happened to you? You're changed." I'm like, "yeah, I know… I don't know. Praise God!" there are no words for what I've experienced this week, but "Praise God." Praise God. Thank you, Jesus, for saving a sinner like me. Thank you, Jesus, for paying that price. You know, I was feeling really bad. Every time I hear and think about Jesus paying the price of our sins, I think 'I don't want anything that I've ever done to be one more hammer getting that nail in deeper to Jesus. I don't want anything that I've done to be another reason why he had to hang on that cross, pay the price in the darkness of Gethsemane, bleeding from every pore. I don't want anything I've done to cause pain to Jesus.' And I think, why is he doing this for everybody? I mean… why?
A) He's the Son of God. He's the only one that could, and B) because of His love for us; he wanted to. He's like "I gotchu." That's Jesus. He's like the ultimate "I gotchu; I got you." And, you know that feeling of 'I got you.'

He works through all of us. Just like that big beam of light going through that human being who helped me to heal. That's my job. Ain't done, sitting on a sofa with a twinkie and drinking out of my sippy-cup. God is in me. God is with me. God has got a reason for me to be here shining that light. That may sound like crazy-person, like "what just happened to Todd? Who is this 'pastor toddymanners?'" It's like I'm full of light. I'm flying. It's been like this for a week for me. How you see me sounding; all of this is on. Praise God. Praise God. That is the faith that transforms you, that makes you just "put on your shoes, put on your cloak, follow Me." I don't need to ask any questions. I don't need to worry if that guard wakes up when I pull my cloak out from under him. If he wakes up, something else will happen. All I need to do is praise God. Follow God. The rest will work out. You find that and you know it; trust it. It don't matter who, from either side or underside, is throwing rocks at you. You know that's what you need to do and you do it, and then it gets bigger. You're like, "Praise God." You move forward; bigger. "Praise God."

You know, one more thing and then I'll wrap it up is that I have, of course, because, part of me is 'well, why is this happening to me? Why am I experiencing this? Why is this all of a sudden? It's like all of the parts are coming together like the house that looked like it was just under construction, looking like it was in total disarray as it was being built, until just right before it's completed and then all the parts just come together and suddenly it's like… there's the house. That's how it feels for me right now. It's like all of these other things that have been bringing parts together and opening doors here, and this goes there, and I'm just moving forward in faith with my shoes and my cloak on, saying 'I don't know what's happening, God, but I know what you want me to do and I'm going to keep on doing that. I'm going to move forward a day at a time and have that feeling of yes, I'm still on that right path and the rest will be taken care of. Coming to where I am this week, thinking why is this happening for me? Why is this immeasurable gift, why is this beautiful experience of healing that I didn't even know I needed, all of a sudden revealing itself at the same time that it is happening, dropping off of me like scales, like soul lesions, spirit lesions just dropping off of me and a transformation that I would have never believed possible, why is this happening to me. There's this saying that, to learn something, a new skill or whatever, you see one… you do one… you teach one. The best way to learn a new skill and have it stay; see one… do one… then teach one. And, as I was thinking about this week, thinking about 'why am I the lucky one?' I mean, God loves all of us the same. Jesus loves all of us the same; paid the price for salvation for all of us the same because He loves us that much. As simple as that. You want to know about love; look to Jesus. You want to know about how to feel love, look to Jesus. To feel like you are worthy of love, look to Jesus. If you feel like you have no love, you look to Jesus. He's got you. He's the ultimate 'I gotchu.' You look to Jesus, you're going to feel the same way I'm feeling right now. You move toward that beam. But, I'm thinking, well what's happening with this with me? And I just got to say: see one… Praise God… do one… look at that beam… Praise God… and go teach one… Praise God. God needs you to have that light shining through you too, just like He was shining through the human who was praying over me.

We talk about the "six degrees of separation." Imagine how many different spirit connections there are, like neurons. All of us are spirits connected in so many different ways. Light one up. See where that path just goes like that. Lit up. Lit up. Lit up. Lit up. Next thing you know, a human being like me that has been broken, angry, bitter… you read any of my old stuff and you'll see; this is a broken human being that is not going to be fixable. There goes that light. Boom… boom… boom… boom. Through all of the spirits around, like a big brain of neurons firing. Next thing you know, somebody's laying their hands on me and I'm feeling the scales of leprosy fall off of my spirit. A transformation that I never could have seen happening. Praise God… Praise God…

I love you a lot. A lot. You find the love of Jesus, you'll know, you'll know the genuine love; this is genuine. I love you very much, and I'm very happy to be a part of that shining light, wherever that takes me. I got my shoes on. I got my cloak on. I don't care who throws rocks at me. I don't care who does whatever they want to me. I know that all I need to do is move forward in this light that I am in right now. Where are we going?

I say all of these things, with the genuine love of my heart. Praise God. That's all. I say this in the name of Jesus Christ, my Lord and Savior, thank you Jesus, amen.

Purple Church of Jesus

♡ for everyone for forever ♡

Purple church of Jesus
Christmas Eve @ 7pm
storynight, cookies & nog

Happenstance the Christmas Moth
December 24, 2025

Who ever heard of something, or someone, as silly-ridiculous as a Christmas moth? Of course no one has, at least not about Christmas specifically, because moths are already everywhere, all the time, not only during Christmas.

Since it's highly unlikely that anyone who is currently reading or hearing this story ever knew, or would ever know, that "Once Upon a Time there was a Christmas moth," it's long past time for that to happen for you. So, keep on reading or listening and you'll see, starting with the question 'what would a Christmas moth's name even be?'

Even saying the words 'Christmas moth' too many times in a row, or too quickly is like trying to whistle with a mouthful of mashed potatoes, so, having an actual name to say, in place of trying to say what he was most famous for, would be a very helpful beginning. Happenstance, if you must know; also goes by Happy for short, and for sounding a little bit less pretentious.

Yep, Happenstance, or Happy as we'll call him more familiarly, because familiarity and family are kind of 'related' in a way. We'll be able to see each other as being a family with him pretty quickly, you'll see, that is, if we would be able to see him at all, even if he was sitting absolutely still, right in front of us both; blending right into whatever he was right next to like a true champ; also, just like practically any other moth would do. Kind of a weird irony (something you'd be surprised that moths are able to see and understand… little known fact) that although our friend's nickname is Happy, he really wasn't; in fact, he hardly ever was, if you want to be completely truthful about it. He could fly around just fine, ate stuff, could get a good day's sleep, made friends sometimes, at least for a little while, and certainly wasn't opposed to that ever happening whenever it didn't or did. Still, he was definitely way more Happenstance than Happy.

"Happy-if-and-when-it-ever-happens" is more like it. Happy is just way easier to say, so he just went along with it anyway and, over time, as you would expect, it became a thing that all of the other moths would automatically attach with his name; without him ever really matching that, in moodiness. Imagine, living long enough to become some sad-sack middle-aged moth who was still stuck, after all of these moth-years, with only ever being known as "Happy." Pretty quickly, you'd see how that could lead to some sorta-severe, moth-level social awkwardness; something that eventually became easier to just avoid altogether. Don't worry. He didn't fly around all sad and stuff all the time. Other moths would just think a certain thing when they'd hear that his name was "Happy", and then, when he wasn't like that after all, well… you know; awkward-silent-moth eye-blinks while quickly computing any other avenues of mutual interest in order to remain at all conversant with each other. Kinda sucked, at least sometimes. If an eavesdropping moth could make a great big fake "boohoo" about something, and then immediately laugh about it, there's the cue.

You may ask, what's the big deal anyway? What could a moth possibly need so much that, when they don't get it, it would bring them unhappiness so predictably? Listen to the laughter of some of the neighborhood butterfly beauties when a moth flies by, especially a moth that looks as ordinary as Happenstance, and then you'll know what's up with what. As petty as it may sound to anyone else, to a moth, seeing a spectacularly beautiful butterfly laughing out loud about your imagined possibilities of reaching even any-level of sub-pretty, one that you'd obviously never be able to achieve; well, that can be pretty demoralizing (another experience that most humans don't realize a moth could ever know anything about; now you do.)

At about the same time that Happenstance had finally had enough of not being the right-kind-of-Happy, and enough of the never-gonna-be nearly pretty enough to be mistaken for ever being even someone else's discarded butterfly, no matter how drunk on milkweed nectar the neighborhood butterflies ever got, even for the nice butterflies who at least wouldn't be laughing about it; he quietly just flitted away the
way that moths usually do.

The thing about stuff that is obvious, is that whatever it is, it wasn't always obvious. There's always that one, discovering-it-time for the first time, on behalf of everybody else, even for the now-obvious stuff. As he was flying away from moth-town, our good friend Happenstance was just about to become one of those happens-once-then-someday-become-obvious ones. He'd have been happy to tell you that story before eventually dying of old age, truly Happy at the end of the day.

It was all because of that Great-Big-Solid-Bright-Star; unmoving, night after night after night. Happenstance had become transfixed by it one night, while all the other moths were busy doing their own busy stuff. After a few nights of staring at it all night long, he'd find himself waking up again, right at dusk, and that Great Big Star would be the first thing that he'd look for; always right there, all big and bright, lodged way up high in the sky in that exact spot where it had been, through the whole night before. Without saying anything to anyone else, because nobody would understand why he'd become transfixed by it anyway, and any delay for any explanations would only become greatly annoying and make everything even more confusing to everyone; he took off from moth-town to find out what was up with that Great Big Star. A star so solid-bright he couldn't think of anything but getting closer to it; as close to it as he could possibly get, no matter how far away it still was. And, while nobody was looking, there he went.

With no way of measuring what time-or-distance is for a moth, Happenstance would never be able to tell anyone how long it took for him to get there, or how many rest stops in the middle of nowhere he'd had to take. His wings though, he would love to tell you about those. You'd think that by going an immeasurable distance, through innumerable, navigationally precarious potentials for missteps, he
would have arrived at that star practically disassembled as a moth; mentally, physically, and in spirit, due to the exhaustion alone. But, in fact, no. The closer that he got to that Great Big Bright Star the stronger and the more determined he felt about getting there. That seed of a feeling that had started somewhere within him, back in moth-town, right from the first time that he saw that Great Big Star, grew within him like it was its very own turbo-engine power-source; created in a moth-version, of course.

By the time that he got to where that Great Big Star had led him, a shamble-barn that immediately felt as home-sweet-home as any place on earth possibly could, ever, his whole moth body spirit and soul were all overflowing with purpose, like some invisible incandescence, even though he'd never have been able to say that word, or tell you what that incandescent purpose was to be, for him. At least not quite yet.

He quietly glided right-up and landed perfectly, right onto the lip of a very old cradle where he saw a brand new cutie-cute human-looking baby, who, even though most human babies are at least a little bit cute, seemed to bring everyone else who had gathered there, all at the same time as Happenstance, to be standing there all mesmerized by the exceptional cutie-cuteness of that baby. Each of them had been brought to that same spot on the planet, with the same unwavering focus and drive that had brought him there, and, even with all the multitudes who had gathered, of every type, and from every corner of everywhere… there was quiet.

Happenstance looked at the baby, as quiet as a moth can be, when a thought or a feeling passed through his mind and his soul in a way that told him, distinctly, that this was not just another one of his internal dialogues that was about to happen. Somehow, this would be a conversation, with this same cutie-cute little baby who was looking directly at him.

"What's the big deal about getting all hung-up on not being as pretty as a butterfly, Happy? There's a whole lot more to stuff than that."

"Umm, I don't know how you know about that, but yeah, it kinda bugs me about why they all got all lucky like that, and I got left with having to reach for hopefully being at least ordinary, on my best days; although, none of that feels like it even matters anymore anyway, because being here with you, right now, is everything that will ever matter to me. And, by the way, for the very first time, coming from anybody, thank you for calling me Happy."

"I'm very glad to hear that, and thank you for that too, because here's the deal, Happy. I always lean-in towards those who don't jump-right-out with all of their beauty-and-purpose already in place, like it had all been pre-packaged that way. I love the less obviously beautiful, who, like you, usually go unseen. Have you ever looked closely at any moth's wings? At your own wings? They're completely fantastic, with an incredible beauty that you would find unimaginable until you stop and look closely enough. Not to be confused with beauty being your purpose; I just wanted to be sure that you noticed that. Your purpose in life, in being here with me today, will last for thousands of years; longer than any beauty I could have offered to you as a butterfly. I know that it's probably weird to hear my baby-Jesus mind conversing with you like this, although, along with knowing a whole bunch about other stuff, knowing that you already know that I mean it literally, when I say that your purpose in being here will last for thousands of years; I'm glad to see that you find that fact puzzling, because that gives me an opportunity to explain it to you. See, it's like this: remember how you felt when you saw that Great Big Star in the sky, turning out to be right above the place where I was born?"

"Yes, my dear cutie-cute baby Lord Jesus, it's like the light from that Big Bright Star was pulling me towards you with a level of magnetism that I had never known existed before. I knew, whatever it meant and whatever it took to do it, I was going to be here with you, exactly like this, exactly like I am right now. I knew that I had to be here, even before knowing what 'here' was, quite yet."

"That, my friend Happy, is exactly what will last for thousands of years because of you, because of the way that you listened, the way that you followed without even having to understand anything about why, quite yet; you just knew, and then, you just did what you knew to do."

"Yes sir, I did that." Happenstance said, through his waving antennae, to baby Jesus, and, without wanting to say it all-out-loud, all the way Happy.

"Because of what you have brought of yourself here, representing all moths from everywhere who will ever be, every moth will now be drawn towards light the same way that you have been drawn to me through my great big star. They won't know how to stop themselves from wanting to be as close to the lights they find, as you have been with mine, on your way to being here with me today. So, from now until the time that we return together again, how-ever-many thousands of moth-years from now that turns out to be, every type and generation of moth being drawn towards light will be a reminder, to anyone who is observant about anything that's even remotely spiritually relevant… I know, big thoughts for a brand new cutie-baby; you see, I've got a whole lot to do in just 33 years, so I had a little bit of a head-start. This moment will be seen through multitudes of human beings observing moths for generations, everywhere; each one fluttering and flittering all around any light that they see, the very same way as you have been here, coming all of this way to find me. This will be our reminder, for generations and generations, to follow the feeling of that Great Big Star, just like you did; right here. There could be no greater purpose than that, my Happy friend, and that is all yours. Your sacred purpose; your incandescence. It did not require having your own set of brightly colored, and, in my humble opinion, overtly attention-seeking wings. It just took you doing what you somehow already knew to do, finding me here today. Hopefully, that will help people begin to wonder, 'well, who was or is that cutie-baby-guy who had that Great Big

Important Star to begin with, and what's the rest of the story of what happened next;' for forever."

"The forever part of forever, huh baby Jesus."

"Yep, the forever part of forever. Thanks for that, my Happy moth-friend."

"Thank you too my tiny, beautiful-baby-friend Jesus. Thank you."

Now, my dear reader, or listener of this Happy Christmas story, when you see a moth flying all around that bright light at your front porch at night, you'll know why that moth is doing all of that flying, right there; reminding you for the moment that you take to remember important stuff.

And, while you're still inside of that moment you can say, right out loud, "thanks, Happenstance." Or, if you choose to, you can just say "thanks, Happy."

…because now, we're family too.

Happenstance

otherwise known as

Happy

the Christmas moth

Purple Church of Jesus

♡ for everyone for forever ♡

One More Upheaval Returns to Earth
January 25, 2026
One More Upheaval Returns to Earth

Hey everybody, pastor toddymanners & AppleJacks here. You're a good boy, AppleJacks. I love you.

Kind of taking a little bit of a hiatus if you will. I will. I'm just having a moment here with my AppleJacks, having a good day. And I think that I don't know, you know, I'm kind of discouraged today because I hope that this wasn't all some uh, Jesus upheaval, you know. Been doing Purple Church of Jesus for oh, how long's it been, AppleJacks? Been about… where are you goin', bud? You going to go play? You can go play. I'll be right here, my friend. I'll be right here. You can go play all you want. Okay, you have fun. You're a good boy. You have fun. I'll be right here. So yeah, that's right. It's you and me always. So, yeah. I've been doing Purple Church of Jesus for almost a year; the real, pointed purpose I felt of being affirming AF for LGBTQIA+ humans who had been kicked out of church… spiritually abused; find their purpose, find God, find their spiritual natures, connect with it and not give a bleep what anybody else has to say aobut that, you know. And in the process of all that, you know, I really did have uh, who knows, I'm still having an upheaval; spiritual Jesus upheaval. Jesus is still my guy; was since the very first Purple Church of Jesus not-a-sermon because I don't preach at people and I don't want to be preached at, but that's what it was called. That's what I still call them. So that part of things remains true, you know, and getting swept-up in the moment.

Oh, there goes the glasses. I just throw glasses. Getting swept up in that, doing Bible study, and there goes my AppleJacks. He's having fun. Ended up getting baptized, saved. December 6th of last year. Just keeping an eye on AppleJacks; and that remains true, will always remain true. That really happened; was a spiritual, like landing on the mothership or the mothership coming back for me kind of thing. That'll always remain true, you know. And I don't know, I just am kind of a… I've been alive long enough to know better than to get too caught up in things. But I still do. Still happens. Happened again and I remain true to my spiritual journey, my spiritual path. But golly, it's hard to not throw that baby out with the bathwater sometimes when you come up against, not against but confronted with, or facing something. What's the word? AppleJacks… playing, having fun with your dog and that's all that matters. That's right.

I'll tell you a joke. What do you get when you cross an insomniac with an agnostic and a dyslexic person, AppleJacks? Do you know? You end up with somebody who lays awake at night and wonders if there really is a dog. Hah. Apple, you having fun? We're going to go off in a second here and go play some more. But I wanted to say a quick hello, to where I'm at, and honor that 'where I'm at' of here. This is a very great place to be with my dog, you know.

The place where I got baptized was uh, you know, come to find out has that same old church policy or dogma, whatever you want to call it. So (big sigh here, hah), don't know who invented it or why. Don't know if it'll ever go away. Marriages. Marriage between "one biological man and one biological woman." That ain't from Jesus, ain't from God, ain't from me, and ain't from you, AppleJacks, huh? You don't believe in that crap. So, sort of in the middle of really separating myself from false dogma and getting closer to my dog. He's the best, huh Apple. AppleJacks and Papa. We're going to go have some fun.

I'm just going through a time right now. Don't know where I'm going to go with Purple Church of Jesus next, but probably the same thing. Just having to remember those rules of engagement and disengagement, with other religions, as they do the thing they do. Got to stir up the masses and get that tithing, pay for them electric bills and all that kind of stuff. The churches have to make sure they're in alignment with what the culture has decided is the most important; because not only will you not find anything in the Bible from Jesus, or really, it'd be hard-scraped to find anything in there from anybody about two men getting married to each other, or a transgender woman and a man getting married to each other. You ain't going to find it. You sure ain't going to find it from Jesus. Not a chance, you know. But they sure like to get it up front and center; make their whatever, you can figure out your own word for it, but you know what mine is. So anyway, want to say, even though I know all those things, getting swept up into it during that part of just getting baptized and saved, and next thing you know, I'm falling into that same old trap. Like, am I always going to fall into that trap every single time? Like, wow, this is the greatest! And then you just get that snag right at the end of, oh… except for that. No, they don't get it either, and not throwing the baby out with the bath water. It's easy to talk about 'don't do that', but when it comes down to 'really don't do that', that's hard. That's hard to not do.

So, I'm connecting with God out here with my dog; my AppleJacks and I out on a little hike, having a great time. And this is our Purple Church. Purple Church of Jesus and AppleJacks my homeboy. Yeah. Because we're together forever. No matter what. No "chat-gbt church dogma, that decided, culturally, would be the most likely way to get the most people to come and cough-up some money and pay them bills" cuz it's all free out here AppleJacks, you and me, that's right.

Purple Church of Jesus will reconvene, I'm sure, as scheduled, last Thursday of the month in January, just going through a thing right now, staying connected with God in my own way, and want to remind everybody else now, don't let them get in-between you and God. Even though that's tough; wears you down. It's tough. Don't let them do it. Don't let them do it. Stay close. Stay connected. God's got you. No matter what other churches decide. They ain't deciding for you or for me or for God or for my AppleJacks. They're deciding for their best interest. They do good at what they do, but they don't get you all the way there. God will get you the rest of the way. All right. I love you. Peace and love from Apple and me. You want to say hi one more time, Apple? Hey, say hi. Say hi, buddy AppleJacks. AppleJacks. That's right. That's our bud. Okay, peace out y'all.

Purple Church of Jesus
greatness
greatness
be what is
for everyone for forever

…in the name of Jesus Christ, amen
…in the name of Jesus Christ, amen
january 12, 2026

Good morning everybody, pastor toddymanners here with Purple Church of Jesus, in Purple Church of Jesus. Last time I made a little video it was with my dog AppleJacks in the park. I was troubled about something coming up with a little bit of a juggle with some church dogma again, and figuring out how that came into alignment, or didn't come into alignment, or how it correlated with my experience with being re-baptized and saved and that little bit of a struggle, you know… I've come through that. So, I want to say good morning and peace and have a little bit of thank God, praise God, that God's with me, and just say praise God.

Do a little bit of reading, little bit of talking about that experience, how I came through that and where I'm at now with that, just because this has been a process, a journey, and I wanted to bring that full circle. So, I wanted to start out by reading from Ephesians about the Whole Armor of God, and that is in Ephesians chapter 6 verses 10 through 18. Yeah, I'm going to just start. Okay. So, finally, my brethren, be strong in the Lord and in the power of his might. Put on the whole armor of God that you may be able to stand against the ways of the devil. For we do not wrestle against flesh and blood, but against principalities, against powers, against the rulers of the darkness of this age, against spiritual hosts of wickedness in the heavenly places. Therefore, take up the whole armor of God that you may be able to withstand in the evil day, and having done all, to stand.

I love that. Stand therefore. I mean, you're standing, so, stand therefore and put on that whole armor of God. That was my words. I added that part. You could probably tell. So, I'll go back again.

So, stand therefore. We're on verse 14. Having girded your waist with truth. There's a good start. Uh, I keep putting in my little; you'll figure it out though. I'm not trying to make my word be the Word of God, but you'll figure out my little edits. I'm not editing them. I'm saying I'm saying Praise God in the middle of the… I'm going to start over.

So again, with 14. Stand therefore, having girded your waist with truth, having put on the breastplate of righteousness, and having shod your feet with the preparation of the gospel of peace, above all, taking the shield of faith with which you will be able to quench all the fiery darts of the wicked one. And, verse 17 now, and take the helmet of salvation. Praise God. And the sword of the spirit which is the Word of God. Praise God. Praying always with all prayer and supplication in the spirit being watchful to this end with all perseverance and supplication for all of the saints.

That is the whole armor of God. You know that there's so many things, when we get troubled, we can come back to, we can find in the Bible that help us through whatever it is. You know, I got this shirt; "… in the name of Jesus Christ", and there's a little "amen." As I was bringing all of that together, with the experience that I was just sharing about in my previous struggle with 'oh, here I am again' with, you know, coming up against a wall of some other church's dogma that isn't congruent with my understanding of the Spirit of God and the power of Jesus Christ in my life; isn't congruent with that. And so, it's like you get these partial truths, and just brilliant light, and then all of a sudden you come up against another wall of just like… no… stop-short… And so, in any struggle in life it's like 'oh, why is life like this, why are things like this happening, and I don't know what to do next and I don't know what to do with this, …in the name of Jesus Christ, amen. Jesus is with you, with me, in the scripture. Put on the whole armor of God. And, as I was thinking about that, coming in misalignment with one-more-time church dogma, thinking you know, "…in the name of Jesus Christ, amen" is not in the name of church-of-that-guy, or, not in the name of you know, cultural homophobia, or in the name of judging others, that includes me in that not-judging-others, or in the name of you-know, make-it-up, all the different distractions that we get in life that are trying to pull us away from our love and our faith and our belief and our relationship, personal relationship with Jesus Christ.

So, coming back to that …in the name of Jesus Christ, amen. I love this shirt because, you know, I want to carry that feeling with me. I want to carry Christ with me. Christ is in my heart. I've been saved. If you haven't had that, then learn about that and feel that in your heart because then you'll know what I'm talking about because it's… you will know what I'm talking about. Carrying that with me, I want to carry with me also what I'm doing; that my actions each day are in the name of Jesus Christ. When I'm whatever-I'm-doing, I want that to be a part of me following Christ, me being of Christ, Christ being with me, in me, and me being an honest representative of Christ. Let your light so shine. You know, love others as I have loved you. If they can see your light so shine, the light of Jesus Christ; seeing the trouble in the world, or having a troubling experience, trying to look at it and go 'where is Jesus in that? And where am I in that, in alignment with Jesus?' and if something is troubling me, like, if I'm hearing something from a church that I can't… I just can't agree with… my experience is different in Christ and they're trying to tell me one thing, convince me of something that I know is not true for me. Being able to say, "Okay, I'm living in the name of Jesus Christ, amen. I'm not living in the name of a church of whatever humans' belief system or dogma. That can be great for them. That can work perfectly for them. That can be exactly right for them. But I'm living in the name of Jesus Christ, amen. And I have a personal relationship with Jesus Christ that both of us understand and respect, and not coming from a place of judgment of or from others; that's up to Jesus.

I think about how it comes up culturally with the LGBTQIA+ stuff, and the reason why I really wanted to make Purple Church of Jesus happen, because it's so common that LGBTQIA+ people are shamed, you know, kicked out of churches or at least made to feel like they're not fully a part of it, or welcomed to it as their authentic selves. Not to say "Oh, ok, well my identity is LGBTQ" but it's not. Our identity is in Christ, and following Christ. Being a gay human, just like being somebody who's whatever, whoever you bring to Jesus; Jesus loves that human, everybody, no matter what. It isn't like, ok, well, except for them or them or them or them… or me. Jesus is right here with me. I don't have to convince anybody of that.

If somebody's looking through, I don't know, the curtains of my soul, the curtains of my life, saying "oh!" with their judgment, or if I'm doing that to others, which I am fully capable of going "oh yeah, you say you're Christian, but what's that crap you're doing in Jesus' name; is that stuff you're doing in the name of Jesus Christ, you're saying that you're Christian?" so I can just jump right onto that judgment and go, "that's incongruent with what I understand as Jesus; well this behavior, you're saying that you're a Christian and doing…" so I'm capable of doing the same thing, going, "oh, let me look through your curtains, the curtains of your soul, make all them judgments happen." I have felt that my whole life from other Christians, other people who say that they follow Jesus and then just hate my guts, or tell me I'm a blasphemer for being gay and talking about Jesus in the same breath and they don't understand my relationship with Jesus and that's just fine. It's not for them.

I've told people before, I have a personal relationship with Christ, and uh, with all respect, this ain't a three-way you know. I don't mean that in a terrible way, but it's like, this is between Jesus and me. You can go find yours. I know mine is true. I've got to not be guilty of the same thing. I've got to make sure that I'm not all in their weeds. If I'm looking through those curtains of their soul, casting judgment, just like what I have felt happen towards me, I've got to make sure I'm seeing the love in there too. I've got to make sure I'm seeing the love. What human element do they have that I'm not seeing past my judgment of them? How can I see that human, as the same human that Christ loves just like Christ loves me, and not cast stones of judgment at that human, who I'm feeling is casting stones at me. And… just know that God's with that person just like God's with me. That person is in their timeline of growth and spirituality and strength and understanding of Christ just like I am with mine. Just being able to be unified in that, without having… 'well, but there's all these filters that you have to pass this test, for me to be able to accept that you're with Jesus' cuz that ain't up to me, ever. Ever. Just like it ain't up to anybody else about me, ever. Ever.

The experience that I had with the church that I didn't… I just couldn't agree with that one part of their dogma… I'm still in connection and in alignment with that church, in a joyful Praise God way, that you would think that, ok, well, close that door; bye. When there's so much other stuff that's just of pure joy, and pure light, pure energy of love with Jesus Christ, feeling his love. I mean, I was re-baptized and saved; had a miracle in that church that I won't ever forget. And so, for me to just go, "well, you know, here in clause B, what did you profess? Nah, nope. That ain't right. So, I'm just going to have to… I talked about it before… throw the baby out with the bath water. All that stuff was great and wonderful and, I felt and I know is true and pure. I'm just going to have to shut the whole door and deny myself of the miracle and truth and joy that I was feeling in that spot with these humans because of this clause 1-a/b whatever that ain't anything to do with Jesus and me."

Being true to myself doesn't mean, okay, let's see how do I put it if I'm being completely honest, which I am, and I mean, honesty is a great way to be because then you don't have to keep track of 'what lies did I say about this and that,' you speak from your heart, speak honestly, speak truth, simple as that, I mean, you're right in the right place in your heart with God. But, you know, people come from a negative place of judgment and they'd be like "Well…" I'm talking about me, here, I'm not talking about, you know, I know other people do it but I'm talking about me, here. If I'm going to be completely honest about, 'well, that just ain't right. What they just, you know, taught about one marriage is one biological male, one biological female'. Aw, it's crap. I'll talk about that a little bit. But if I'm going to be honest about, "hey, that's uh, you know, I can't agree with that and that's kind of baloney." I've got to also be honest about the stuff that is working and is beautiful and true and pure and of God. A solid feeling of the Holy Spirit entering my body and me being baptized, saved, miracles that happened all in alignment with that, the human experiences that I've had with people all along the way in that journey, from before and with and continuing in Christ.

If I'm going to be honest, all the way honest, I can't just say, "Oh, well, there's that thing. Uh, nope, maybe for you, but nope. I don't agree." Be honest about that. I got to also be honest about all of this beauty and truth that really is happening and really did happen, and not just go, ok, because of that, all of this follow God, follow Christ means, hey, we're all in different places with our understanding of God, of Jesus Christ.

That's the beauty of it. I get to have a personal relationship with Christ that only Jesus and I are a part of. So, Jesus ain't going to be shutting the door on somebody just because of this one thing or that thing or that thing. And you got to see the whole beauty and truth and joy and Praise God; the rest will figure it out with everybody, with all of us, me included. Being LGBTQIA+ affirming AF, loving God, praising God may not be something anybody can understand who is stuck in that dogma. That's alright, because, what is it; this vin diagram, or whatever, where you have the circles that have some kind of overlap and some kind of parts that don't. Our overlap part, of where we are, the congregation that I've been going to, the people that I've met there, the overlap part of what we've got is just pure and beautiful and true loving God, praising God, loving Jesus, feeling the Holy Spirit enter us and be amongst us in congregation with God and in love and worship with God. That part of that overlap is beautiful and true. And, just because there's this one part on the side, guess what? Every one of us has stuff like that. Whatever it's about, we can have an understanding with God and know where we are with God and where we need to be with God without all the rest of that BS; purity that we share with others in worship of God. We don't have to throw all that out because of that little sliver.

Yeah, I'll continue to be LGBTQIA+ affirming AF, and that was kind of the heartbreak part of the experience I went through, was that my marriage, with my wife, such a beautiful marriage we have a strong, strong marriage. Married 11 and a half years. You know, when we got together, I just immediately knew this is what I've been; really, this is love. This is beautiful. I love this human being that is now in my life and I want to marry this human being that is now in my life. It's 11-1/2 years we got married on this happiest day of my life. I've talked about it before. Three of the happiest, I've got three happiest days of my life. The day I went on a mission, with the Church of Jesus Christ of Latter Day Saints when I was 19 years old; the day I went and did that, served that mission, fulltime mission. The day I got married to my beautiful wife, transgender woman of color, beautiful, beautiful human being. Our marriage. Our wedding day, the 11-1/2 years since then. And the day I was saved; re-baptized and saved. You know, these three days I will not deny. No one can take those from me. And so, the sadness of what I just experienced, with being re-baptized and then finding out, you know, I shouldn't… I'm glad that I didn't look ahead of time, because then I would have denied myself the whole experience with the church, and going through that Bible study for a few months, and because I would have just judged ahead of time, okay well, we're not in alignment so I can't go there. I can't do that; I would have missed all of this, that turned out to be one of my three happiest days of my life.

To come to the other side of that, and find that dogma that I couldn't find a place for in my heart, and my spirit, and my understanding of Jesus Christ and what Jesus wants for me, and wants for all of us, to just be able to follow him in love with each other, you know, with love of the example of

Jesus Christ, how Christ loves. You know that keeps it really simple.

That beautiful experience I had with being re-baptized and saved; you know that was a real act of faith for my wife to allow me, or, not like she would have been able to allow me or not allow me. This is the path that I've been pulled toward, been growing in, have been flourishing in, and have felt strength from. So, she wouldn't have been able to stop that, just like, when she approached me and said "I'm a transgender human, and I hope that we can stay together in our marriage" right at the beginning of our marriage. I mean, of course, I love her. Of course we're staying strong and true together in our marriage, but she was nervous about how I would feel about her identifying as a transgender woman, and how that would impact our marriage. Whatever had happened in that part of it, she's a transgender woman. That's who she is. It doesn't have anything to do with whether or not I can stay married with her because of that. That's who she is. That's who she is.

You know we can stay together in our marriage, right at the beginning of our marriage. I mean, of course, I love her. Of course, we're staying strong and true together in our marriage, you know, but she was nervous about how I would feel about her identifying as a transgender woman and how that would impact our marriage. Whatever had happened in that part of it, she's a transgender woman. That's who she is. Doesn't have to do with whether or not I can stay married with her because of that. That's who she is. Us being able to go through that together, me in support and just seeing the beauty of her transition as a transgender woman is one of the miracles of my life. And I, you know, anybody who either is transgender and is transitioning, or a spouse or close friend or loved one, family member who is able to experience that transition with them and support and just being a part of that with them, you'll see just incredible beauty every step of the way affirmed. Yes, this is exactly the right way to move forward for this human who I love. Every moment we moved forward together, I saw her brightness and joy expand and expand and expand. Her identity of who she is in herself just getting bigger and more beautiful, more beautiful, more joyful.

It really has been amazing, and her, being nervous about 'are we going to be able to stay together now that I'm identifying as transgender human, transgender woman of color', I was immediately like, yeah, let's. I mean, we don't know what we're… how to do that, but I love you. I'm not leaving this marriage because of you becoming more of who you are. you are who I love, why would I leave because of you becoming more of who I love. So, let's find out how we do that as we move forward. And it's just gotten bigger and more wonderful and happier and every step of the way.

Me now, sort of having this transition reaffirming my faith really, you know, strongly, with my understanding and my alignment with Jesus Christ in an out-loud way and not being ashamed of that; being proud of that, being excited about that, being that light on the hill, you know, for LGBTQIA+ people. That can feel like a threat to some because of the spiritual abuse we've experienced, be like, "Well, uh-oh, this friend of mine…" or, husband in our case, you know, my wife's husband, me, "I hope that that doesn't harm our marriage," that I am following Christ, loving Christ, being re-baptized and saved, praying that I can be of service to God. Put me where you want me, God. Tell me what you want me to do. I want to move forward with you in spirit of wherever you want me to go. And me being able to hear that and see that and follow that and move forward with that is a scary experience for somebody who is in a LGBTQIA community because we've all been raised in a place of "we don't belong and we're hated and we should be kicked out" and it's incongruent with Christianity and all that hatred, all that shame, all that disgust, all that abandonment, all that throwing us out. Automatically that has become so ingrained that we would immediately think of ourselves or our loved ones, including our spouses, "uh-oh the closer you get to that that's a danger to our marriage that's a danger to our friendship that's a danger to how we understand each other and I don't know if we'll be able to remain together in friendship" you know, and if you're going toward Christ how is that going to affect, in my case, my wife and I. How's it going to affect our marriage?

I got to say it is different but the same, in me having faith in our marriage and love for my wife when she came out as a transgender human and asked if I wanted to remain married with her as she transitioned through that and, you know, hoping that we'd stay together and be able to be, you know, strong together still, and us moving forward in that direction and staying strong and that becoming better and better and better. It's similar in a way to her seeing me go through this process right now. And how sad it is, to come through that, and then find "Oh," one more time.

"Oh, one-biological…"

Jesus. Jesus, I love you. Jesus ain't ever walking around in Bible times saying, "you know, let's talk about one biological male and one biological female." Jesus doesn't talk like that. He don't; he didn't ever. And so, that being such a prominent, pervasive sentiment in what call themselves "Christian" churches, Christian in so many ways, but misses that one, every time, almost every time.

You know, that being so pervasive that it would immediately feel like a threat to any LGBTQIA human. Therefore, suicide rates, alcoholism, isolation, etc., etc. etc. It's a long list and included in that list would be a threat to the marriage I have of beauty and strength with my beautiful wife, just implied across the board without anybody even having to talk about it.

Everybody who knows my wife and I know we have a strong, beautiful, happy, solid marriage flying in the multicolored universe together. Beauty travels between us. Everybody who knows us knows that that is us. That's our marriage is beautiful. Still strong, happy. I'm serious. It's so great. So, to just think in the back of anybody's mind, including my wife's mind, worry of, you know, me re-strengthening my relationship with Jesus Christ. Is that going to be a threat to our marriage? And gosh, that's so sad. And, heck no. No way. No way.

I talk about love being my fireplace, and how, you know, when I was excommunicated and things felt like they were falling off, being chipped away from me, my everything I loved was, you know, everything I believed, everything I understood about God and about life, about myself was being chipped away, broken, and it came down to my fireplace; my place of love. Hurricanes happen, tornadoes, everything terrible, you know, natural disasters flatten all these houses and then you see the news coverage later and all you see are these fireplaces where houses once were. There's timber crashed everywhere on the ground and you see fireplace, fireplace, fireplace; still standing.

My fireplace is love. I said, "Okay, nope. You can take anything else. You can chip it away. You can say I don't get it. You can say I'm not worthy. You know, lose all that stuff. But my fireplace is mine and hanging onto that, and that being a source of strength for me." Now, with my revitalization in Christ, feeling the spirit of God in me, that's my fireplace. I mean, Jesus; Wow. Just like my shirt. You know those times get dark, you can't see the way, just look to Jesus. Follow-follow me. That's all he says. Follow me. Nobody's going to take away my Jesus. A friend of mine was cracking up because I was going through that moment, and then came to the conclusion, like you can throw all the rainbow-hate you want all the way to judgment day. Nobody's going to chase me away from my Jesus. Nobody gets to do that. Finding, wow, that's really part of my fireplace, too.

Jesus Christ and love, together. This is my fireplace. You ain't going to take that away. My marriage is full of love. You think you're going to be able to come in and cast judgment and say, "Well, either Jesus or your marriage?" No. Because, guess what? My marriage is strong, solid with love, just really genuine, pure, just joyful. And Jesus; you know it. If you know Jesus, if you have a relationship with Jesus, you know it. You know it. That's why people are raising their hands. They're like, "Oh, this is so great. Joy, just strength. Jesus." If you know that feeling, you cannot deny it. You know it. They're like, "Praise God." You get these two together. Love and Jesus. Love… my fireplace. I said, "You ain't going to take it." Jesus…my fireplace. You put those together. Wow. The whole world can do any crazy-crazy thing it wants to do. Solid. I'll follow Christ. I'll follow God. I'll feel that Spirit fill me; fill me up. And I'm just asking God, where do you want to take me? What do you want me to do? God needs what I have to bring to the world. For the longest time, I didn't think that was true.

For the longest time, I thought I just took up space and I really needed to just check out. You know, people talk about "the gay lifestyle." Yeah, it's like "people die young of that because, well, AIDS" which, you know, we got ignored; hated even through that. That's when our community really stood together strong cuz nobody had our backs but us. Our family members became the brotherhood and sisterhood of our LGBTQIA+ community, who had been rejected by everyone. We found each other and found our community together and… seeing each of us just… I mean… it was nightmarish. Everybody dying… everybody. It was just like, we were all going to die. So many… just, so many… and the world didn't care at all. Some; some did, but we came together in community and you know, nobody's going to take away my ability to love or feel love from any source.

That is Jesus speaking. When I feel love, I have my heart with love, that's Jesus speaking. You can cast any judgment you want. That's the language of Jesus. Love is… they say "love the sinner, hate the sin," which instead is like a passive-aggressive way of saying that you can still just cast judgment anyway; you're still just throwing rocks at that person through some clichéd phrase. Still the same. I heard a phrase: "love the believer, not the belief." That's pretty funny.

Anyway, affirming AF, LGBTQIA+ loving Christ can be the same. My love for the people of the church that I had been going to, and continue to go to; in fact, going to go again this morning for a prayer service. You know, just because of that clause 1-A, whatever, great, you believe that way, go ahead. But I'm going to be here in the presence of God with the love of Christ in my heart without casting judgment on others just like I don't want it to be cast on me, and really just praising God, and the love of what God has done for us, what Jesus has done for us. You can figure the rest out, but… I wanted to… you know what…?

I'm going read one more thing from the book of Acts, at the end of the book of Acts. This describes to me Purple Church of Jesus. I mean, when Paul was writing this in the book of Acts, he wasn't going, "Oh, you know, there's going to [clears throat] be this Purple Church of Jesus." Of course, but this is in alignment with how I feel about Purple Church of Jesus. It's at the very end of Acts, and we're looking at chapter 28 starting with verse 25. And he says, "So when they did not agree among themselves, they departed after Paul had said one word." This is in in quotes. The Holy Spirit spoke rightly through Isaiah the prophet to our fathers, saying, "Go to this people and say, "Hearing you will hear and shall not understand, and seeing you will see and not perceive. For the hearts of this people have grown dull. Their ears are hard of hearing and their eyes they have closed. Lest they should see with their eyes and hear with their ears lest they should understand with their hearts and turn so that I should heal them. Therefore, let it be known to you that the salvation of God has been sent to the Gentiles and they will hear it. And when he had said these words, the Jews departed and had a great dispute amongst themselves. Then Paul dwelt two whole years in his own rented house and received all who came to him, preaching the kingdom of God and teaching the things which concern the Lord Jesus Christ with all confidence, no one forbidding him.

That's so great. That gives me goosebumps to read that. It's so great, you know. And he's saying, "Yeah, this salvation of God has been sent to the Gentiles and they will hear it, you know." And in the Bible times, it's like "the Gentiles? No!" It's scandalous.

I know he's not talking about LGBTQIA people when he says "the Gentiles", but it makes me feel that parallel of, "Oh, but no, the LGBTQIA, they're bad, bad, bad, bad, bad, shame, shame, hate, hate" all that stuff that makes us feel so terrible about ourselves, and makes other people hate us 'because Jesus.' That stuff is such crap. I just draw that parallel with… "Yeah. Even for the Gentiles, even for the LGBTQIA people, we're going to be out there preaching, loving God, helping them find the spirit of God, helping them receive the spirit of God in themselves, in their hearts." Doesn't mean, "Oh, you're a gentile? Oh… sorry"; like we feel from within LGBTQA community. Oh… wait. You know, the only way you're entering is if you're like, "Don't notice. Don't notice any of my humanity. Let me just sneak in the back door here."

No.

And when he had said these words, the Jews departed and had a great dispute amongst themselves. Then, Paul dwelt two whole years in his own rented house. Purple Church of Jesus. This is so great. I know he's not talking about that, but that's how I feel here in Purple Church of Jesus.

Then Paul dwelt two whole years in his own rented house and received all who came to him, preaching the kingdom of God and teaching the things which concern the Lord Jesus Christ with all confidence.
No one forbidding him. It ain't some "church of Joe Schmo" or "church of yada yada yada." I'm following Jesus Christ. I can feel the power and love and salvation of Jesus Christ in a church. But that does NOT make that church Jesus Christ.

There's One.

Jesus Christ is living in my heart right now. I can go to another church and feel Jesus Christ with His happy-heart beating for us in that church; any church. But, when I exit that church, and if that church doesn't come into 100% alignment with what I believe, it doesn't mean that Jesus says, "Okay, well, see ya, I'll be here when you get back." He's still right here with me. Right here. Siempre juntos y siempre cresciendo. See?

So yeah, I'm in a good place; great place. I've found how to sort through that turmoil in my head like, "Oh, here I am again, swirling, trying to understand." I think that brings us forward in strength, when we go through experiences like that, we go, "How do I find Jesus in this experience? How do I follow Jesus in this experience? Where do I go next with this experience loving Christ? Going where Christ wants me to go. Go in my heart, in my body, in my spirit, in my community." Pray. Put on that whole armor of God. Read every one of those things that are included in the armor of God. Follow Christ. Follow that light.

I love you. Thank you for walking through that process with me; to explain where all that went. Still strong in God. Still strong in Christ. Moving forward. We'll have our next Purple Church of Jesus on the last Thursday of the month like we always do. I think it's on the 29th of January. So, peace and love. Rock on.

Thank you, God. Praise God. I say these things right here, in the name of Jesus Christ. Follow him. When you're confused, when you're struggling, when you're sad, when you're lonely, when you're depressed, people are throwing their stuff at you; try not to throw any back, just shine that light, in the name of Jesus Christ. Amen. Peace and love.

Purple Church of Jesus
greatness
greatness
be what is
for everyone for forever

Jesus, Martin Luther King, and Shadrach at Purple Church of Jesus

January 19, 2026

Hello everybody, pastor toddymanners here with Purple Church of Jesus, and I wanted to do just a brief not a sermon today, honoring Martin Luther King Day and all that has resonated still through today about the civil rights movement, that he helped to propel, through his inspiration and nonviolence, and that we still gather from what he said during that volatile time; this still resonates now and gives us a really solid strong example of accomplishing change with the civil rights movement. I mean, what existed before the civil rights movement towards people of color, African-Americans, black people, now you've got… they want to hang up the Ten Commandments in the classrooms to show "the origins of our country." Well, hey, if that's the imperative, "to show the origins of our country" then don't forget to include how people treated black people at the beginning of this country, slaves, the Civil War… lynchings… Jim Crow laws… people justifying all manner of heinous activity toward black people, even while they were still preaching from the Bible. White people preaching from the Bible while treating black people that way. And, if you're think that things in our day don't ever carry that same, deeply racist mentality, then you're willfully not paying attention.

I find it so inspiring and so incredible and so just fascinating that during that time; listen to gospel music. I mean, these are people who were so abused, misused, killed, just every horrible thing you can imagine happening to black people in the origins of our nation, which, you know, I already said it, you know, put all <u>that</u> up on the walls of the school kids classrooms if you if your origin of the nation is what? But no, that would be too woke; that would hurt the feelings of white kids who we can't ever let know what the true "origins of our country" were like. But, gospel music during that time; listen to it. It's amazing. I mean, the strength of love and how people made it through that time, keeping their faith intact, their love of God intact, their love for Jesus Christ, the Lord intact through song. Listen to the music. Gospel music. It's just really… it's fascinating… incredible. People did not lose heart even though you can't imagine getting through that time without losing heart. I find that so inspiring.

With Martin Luther King Day being today, I wanted to do a little bit of a not-a-sermon honoring him. And I wanted to start out by reading from Daniel, about Shadrach, Meshack and Abednego. And this is Daniel chapter 3. Why don't I start at about this King Nebuchadnezzar guy? I'll start with uh yeah verse 9; chapter 3:9.

They spoke and said to King Nebuchadnezzar, "Oh king, live forever. You, oh king, have made a decree that everyone who hears the sound of the horn, flute, harp, liar, and sultery in symphony with all kinds of music shall fall down and worship the gold image. And whoever does not fall down and worship shall be cast into the midst of a burning fiery furnace. There are certain Jews whom you have set over the affairs of the province of Babylon. Shadrach, Meshack, and Abednego. These men, oh king, have not paid due regard to you. They to the king. They do not serve your gods or worship the gold image which you have set up. Then Nebuchadnezzar in a rage and fury gave the command to bring Shadrach, Meshack, and Abednego.

"Bible times." This… yeah, we're living in "Bible times." If you haven't heard me say that, we're living in Bible times. So, this King Nebuchadnezzar is in a rage, and furious, gave the command to bring Shadrach, Meshach, and Abednego. So they brought these men before the king. Nebuchadnezzar spoke, saying to them, "Is it true, Shadrach, Meshack, and Abednego, that you do not serve my gods or worship the gold image which I have set up?" See, that's the thing about tyrants and authoritarians. They've got to make sure everybody does like they do, right? It's a threat if you don't. It's a threat, you know. Whereas truth stands on its own. It is the truth that shall set you free. It doesn't mean "okay well, you have to believe this and do this or else I'm going to have to throw you in the fire." It means… here is the truth. It doesn't require some tyrant or authoritarian to make you bend to his will. Nebuchadnezzar spoke, saying to them, "Is it true, Shadrach, Meshack, and Abednego, that you do not serve my gods or worship the gold image which I have set up? Now if you are ready, at the time you hear the sound of the horn, these are the rules of the king, in symphony with all kinds of music and you fall down and worship the image which I have made good. He's saying, "If you do like I say, great." You know, compliance. All you have to do is do what they say and everything will be okay, right? [clears throat] No one will get hurt. Bible times. All you have to do is do what they say. He says to them, "But if you do not worship, you shall be cast immediately into the midst of a burning fiery furnace, and you'll be to blame for that. And who is the God who will deliver you from my hands?" Shadrach, Meshack, and Abednego answered and said to the king, "Oh Nebuchadnezzar, we have no need to answer you in this matter." Ain't that great?

Bible times. They're knocking on the door. I don't need to show you my ID. I don't need to tell you my name. I can walk down the street, a U.S. citizen, going from place to place without having to worry about being stopped by someone who has no warrant, no charges against me, and being thrown into a van. I love this boldness. This is in Daniel 3:16. Shadrach, Meshack, and Abednego answered and said to the king, "Oh Nebuchadnezzar," almost like, 'Oh, bless your heart.' Oh Nebuchadnezzar, we have no need to answer you in this matter. If that is the case, our God whom we serve is able to deliver us from the burning fiery furnace, and he will deliver us from your hand, O king. But if not, let it be known to you, O king, that we do not serve your gods. Nor will we worship the gold image which you have set up." They put a steak in the ground. They're like, well, why would we just follow the lies? Why would we just endorse your lies? I ain't going to chase that moving target. Start down that rabbit trail of chasing lies and saying, "Oh, that's true. That's true. That's true." Or, just not saying anything. Huh? Stand True. Stand Solid. Truth will set you free. That's it. John 8:31-32. Okay. Okay, so they're shoved into the fire. Nebuchadnezzar was full of fury. He's a mad king. And the expression on his face changed toward Shadrach, Meshack, and Abednego because they weren't bending to his will. They weren't going to do what he said. Just cuz he said it didn't make it. Bible times. He spoke and commanded that they heat the furnace seven times more than it is usually heated; kind of melt them. And he commanded certain mighty men of valor who were in his army. Oh, he's got people that are going to do whatever he says because they're scared of him; to bind Shadrach, Meshack, and Abednego and cast them into the burning fiery furnace.

These men were bound in their coats, their trousers, their turbans, and their other garments, and were cast into the midst of the burning fiery furnace. Therefore, because the king's command was urgent, and the furnace exceedingly hot, the flame of the fire killed those men who took up Shadrach, Meshack and Abednego.

So, the guys that took them to throw them in the fire, they themselves caught on fire. Those little foot-soldiers for the king, that were doing his will, <u>they</u> were the ones that caught on fire, just by taking Shadrach, Meshack, and Abednego there. And these three men, Shadrach, Meshack, and Abednego, fell down, bound into the midst of the burning fiery furnace.

Then, King Nebuchadnezzar was astonished, and he rose in haste, and spoke, saying to his counselors, "Did we not cast three men bound into the midst of the fire?" They answered and said to the king, "True, O king"; like they'd say and would do anything; but yes, be sure to say yes to whatever he'd said anyway. Bible times. They said, "True, O king. Look," he answered. "I see four men loose walking in the midst of the fire, and they are not hurt. There's four in there." Who's that fourth? You got to think about that for a little bit, huh? Walking. So, he said, "I see four men loose, walking in the midst of the fire, and they are not hurt." and the form of the fourth is like the son of God.

Then, Nebuchadnezzar went near the mouth of the burning fiery furnace and spoke saying, "Shadrach, Meshack, and Abednego, servants of the most high God." Look who just had a conversion. The same guy that was throwing them in the fire 10 seconds ago. Well, or however long ago. Shadrach, Meshack, and Abednego, servants of the most high God. Come out and come here. Then Shadrach, Meshack, and Abednego came from the midst of the fire, and the administrators, governors, and the king's counselors gathered together, and they saw these men on whose bodies the fire had no power. The hair of their head was not singed, nor were their garments affected, and the smell of fire was not on them. Nebuchadnezzar spoke, saying, "Blessed be the God of Shadrach, Meshack, and Abednego, who sent his angel, and delivered his servants who trusted in him. And they have frustrated the king's word and yielded their bodies that they should not serve nor worship any god except their own god."

That's so cool, huh? That's so cool. True. True. So true to their beliefs, so true to their understanding, so true to God. They're like, "Okay, you big bully. You want to throw us in the fire? Okay, but we're not going to start doing what you say just cuz you're trying to scare us."

"Therefore, I make a decree that any people," this is Nebuchadnezzar, "still having had a conversion after seeing them come out of that furnace unharmed." This is Nebuchadnezzar saying there on verse 29 of chapter 3 still [clears throat] "therefore I make a decree that any people, nation or language which speaks anything amiss against the God of Shadrach, Meshack and Abednego shall be cut in pieces and their houses shall be made an ash heap because there is no other god who can deliver like this." So, he's still like, "Oh, now you have to do it like I say or else I'm going to burn you and chop up your house." In other words, he hadn't gotten all the way there yet. Hah. Yeah. He's got a way to go. We're all a work in progress, right? Hah.

Then the king promoted Shadrach, Meshack, and Abednego in the
province of Babylon. Then, he has this dream starting in the beginning of chapter 4. Nebuchadnezzar the king to all people, nations, and languages that dwell in all the earth. Peace be multiplied to you. I thought it good to declare the signs and wonders that the most high God has worked for me. This is Nebuchadnezzar. How great are his signs and how mighty his wonders. His kingdom is an everlasting kingdom and his dominion is from generation to generation. So that's the conversion of Nebuchadnezzar, after witnessing Shadrach, Meshack, and Abednego staying

true to themselves, staying true to God; staying alive. Fourth angel, I guess, in there with them, talking with them. Probably they said the fourth is the son of God. Maybe it was Jesus. I don't know. Doesn't go any further into detail than that.

I think it's really amazing that the conversion of Nebuchadnezzar came from them standing true to their faith. You've got to wonder, if they had just been one more of the bajillion examples of people who had caved into that fear from that king, who wanted you to worship his gold or listen to the music that he wants you to listen to, and bow down and worship him; do things his way. Otherwise… you're thrown into the fire. You know, if they had been the bajillionth iteration of that happening, there would have been no change for Nebuchadnezzar; no sorta-conversion. Probably not, anyway. Maybe something else would have happened later on. But if they had just said, "Okay, well, what do you want us to do? We'll be in compliance. You know, don't harm us. We'll do whatever you say. You know, just uh tell us what you want us to do, you know, is it ok to open the glovebox to get my ID? We'll keep our hands uh where you can see them and uh won't reach for our identification until you say so, which you don't probably don't want to see anyway, just don't get suspicious of what am I doing with my hands when I'm just trying to give you the documentation you said you wanted and then, you using that as "a threat" then I'm dead. This fear thing is a powerful tool for tyrants to use.

I often wonder how, if you've got faith in God, faith in Jesus Christ, if you've been saved, if you're following Christ, what is there to be afraid of? I mean; He's everything. He's, you know, all powerful, sovereign, you're saved; what threat is there that can exceed that in risk? I mean Shadrach, Meshack, and Abednego, they had already experienced that. They knew that, even though this is from the Old Testament, I mean, they knew that in their hearts that, well, why would I just bend to your will, praise your gods or your gold or, you know, whatever it is you're saying you want me to do, just so I can be safe, when I'm already saved? I don't need to be afraid, you know. My life is already eternal. Even if you get thrown into a fire and you light me on fire and I burn into ash, like he was threatening, and afterwards had his little half-conversion; terrible things happen. Guess what? I still already have eternal life. You don't have power over me beyond the grave. You can take my body, but you cannot take my spirit, my soul; you can do whatever you want, but I mean, I've already got everlasting life. I've already got salvation.

The fear tactics that are used sometimes really astonish me, how powerful they can be. It is evidence to me of people who have not found
enough of the love of Jesus Christ; salvation. Like, what is there to be afraid of? Sure, you want to not just walk in front of a car and get hit, but at the same time, letting fear drive your life or rule your life and your decision-making process is probably not evidence of having faith. Faith over fear. This fear tactic that's used is really effective.

It's almost like the parting of the Red Seas. You've got people who are going to be following this King Nebuchadnezzar type of worship, whatever he says to think or do, day-by-day. you know, whatever it is, is going to change and it's going to be another opportunity or disaster for you personally around you showing your fealty; doing whatever he and his whims-of-the-day say. Be in compliance so you don't have to be afraid. On one side, you've got people that would be "just do whatever he says, do whatever he says, do whatever he says, just keep me safe" where Jesus is standing there going, "Hey," I mean, literally with his arms out saying, "Hey, I got you. Don't lose that." And then on the other side, you know, calling it out and saying, "Hey, that's um kind of BS. Tell me I have to worship your gods or worship your music, musical instruments, whatever that those were." Uh-uh. I don't believe that. I'm not going to do that. Getting thrown in the fiery furnace… we all live in the same world. Your federal government decides they need to shoot you in the face cuz you're not doing what they say; making up an excuse for why they did that, later, you know, tail wagging the dog all the way across the country like, "Oh, we'll justify everything we need to later, just do what you're told. You know, we'll make up the reasons why we had to do these terrible things to people later, and people will fall in line. See you in church." So, you divide that. You divide everybody that way; people on one side afraid that they're going to lose power or position or proximity to power or possessions or safety because they're going to get thrown right in the fiery furnace too if they say "nah, that's not how I believe; I'm not going to worship all your gods even though you're a big scary person with lots of power that could throw me in a fiery furnace. I'm going to show up and call it out, speak truth to power, all that kind of stuff." And then you see every day what happens. People's front doors being busted down and they're being pulled out of their houses in their underwear while their kids are inside crying and trying not to raise enough attention that, you know, guns get aimed at them too… by the government.

King Nebuchadnezzar; that power tyranny, authoritarianism. I mean, it just it clears a path on both sides of that through fear, then marches right up through the middle. Says, "Okay, I'm going to just keep on doing anything." Not "I" obviously, but whoever that is, Nebuchadnezzar marched right up through the middle of all that, cleared a path by using fear on both sides, keeping

people out of the way. Do a smash and grab for whatever you want. Who's going to stop you? Just keep them afraid. Keep everybody divided and afraid. March right up through the middle so you never know what is going to happen. You just keeping your faith, stand your ground, saying I don't have to bend my will to somebody else's gods or their tyranny just because I'm afraid, because I don't need to be afraid. First of all, I'm saved. Jesus Christ paid the price on the cross for my salvation. Redemption, eternal life is achieved through the experience that I had of baptism, being saved, receiving the gift of the Holy Spirit. Why would I need to be afraid of some schoolyard
Bully, even if he's threatening my life with a fiery furnace? Okay. So, go ahead. I mean, I'm not going to say that I'm going to be the guy that's going to be walking around a fiery furnace with an angel and walk out later without being singed. I mean, I'm probably mortal. I'd probably melt, but that's my body. My soul, and my spirit are eternal already. I don't need to be afraid.

Starting that out with the story of Shadrach, Meshack, and Abednego, on Martin Luther King Day, honoring and celebrating the example that Martin Luther King, really the whole civil rights movement, people in authority now don't even want you to talk about it, in schools or whatever. 'Don't get inspired to try to change the world, ever, in a nonviolent way like Dr. Martin Luther King because then comes "the power."' We know the 'scary people' have got to hold onto the power. So, of course they don't want to celebrate MLK too much cuz he's a game changer, world changer, still is.

There's this quote from him that is really famous, that I want to bring into this, that he had written while he was in the Birmingham jail.

He said, "Injustice anywhere is a threat to justice everywhere." One of his most well-known quotes, injustice anywhere is a threat to justice everywhere. You turn on the TV or social media or whatever, however you keep track of what's going on in the world right now, and you tell me if you see any injustice, you know, take your political blinders off, take your 'seeking for proximity to power or more power or more money' or whatever those trinkets of Nebuchadnezzar were that he was using. Take all of that away. Just look at human beings. What we're experiencing, right now, without all of those blinders or filters or conditions or anything; just another child of God walking through the day, not doing anything wrong. Next thing you know, they're getting pulled out of their house in their underwear by a whole bunch of militarized thugs with weapons aimed at them, at that person and that person's family, pulling them out of the house in the snow. Just take off all the blinders, you know, take off all the filters. Just look at that human, or any other of the gajillions of examples we're seeing every day. Look at that human as a child of God and ask yourself, are you seeing any injustice? Because injustice anywhere is a threat to justice everywhere.

Considering that "injustice anywhere is a threat to justice everywhere" I look at how they demonize LGBTQs, especially transgender humans, saying that "oh there's this executive order and now there's no such thing as a transgender human anymore." I mean, what person has that level of power, whether or not they're voted into any office, to just sign a piece of paper and say "okay, now this whole group of people no longer exists
cuz I decided." Come on. That is crap. You've got to call it what it is. It's boloney. You don't have one person that can just decide, okay, none of you exist. And by the way, even though that whole group of people that doesn't exist now,

because of this piece of paper I signed, we're going to persecute all of them even though they don't exist now. Go after all of them. Call them all kinds of bad names; worse names now.

Now you know. Don't pretend that you don't. You are living in the same world as me. "I signed a piece of paper. Now we're going to go after that minority. Okay. Now that shook things up enough, kept people afraid and kept quiet pretty good. Now we're going to go after this other minority, now this other minority." We've seen the history of the world 100,000 times. You don't even have to look back very far.

No. Injustice. Anywhere. It's a threat to justice everywhere.

They're not going to just, like the richest people in the world are not going to stop wanting more money and more power. People who have the most power; do you think they're going to just be satisfied one day and say, "Okay, well, now we're done. We have all the power we need. We have all the, you know, land we need and money we need, we've taken other countries or done whatever. So, we're good. We're sated." That ain't ever going to happen. It's going to be more and more and more. We've got to stand up. Shadrach, Meshack, and Abednego understood that. I ain't going to bend my will to some tyrant who wants me to believe him, whatever his flavor of the day 'believe and defend whatever he says''; just showing fealty, while calling it loyalty. If so, you're not going to have any integrity; just flying through the winds of a flatulent fascist.

First of all, you're not going to be able to hang on to the truth because there stops being any such thing; second of all, cuz you get stuck with swimming in whirlpools of lies. You don't know upside-down from right-side-up anymore and it will all be something different tomorrow anyway. “Bible times.”

One more quote I wanted to bring forward from Dr. Martin Luther King, on Martin Luther King Day, is about non-violence cuz gosh, things are escalating, huh? Don't get pulled into it.

He says, "It is no longer a choice, my friends, between violence and nonviolence. It is either nonviolence or non-existence. Non-cooperation with evil is as much a moral obligation as is cooperation with good." So just standing by, doing nothing, is not what we're called for. Well, that's Martin Luther King, but Jesus was saying basically the same stuff. I wanted to go to Matthew chapter 8; 8, 9 and 10 are all about leading with faith. Faith comes first. Don't wait for the evidence and then decide. Move forward with faith. Faith over fear, through Matthew 8, 9 and 10, he's working miracles; the woman who wouldn't stop bleeding for like 12 years. She touched the hem of his garment and was healed. He looked at her and she was like, "Thank you." And he said, "It's your faith that has healed you."

The guy whose daughter had had died. His faith is what was able to bring her back from death. People being blind, being healed. There are all of these examples in these few chapters. Someone who couldn't speak, speaking, and starting here with chapter 9 verse 32 when the mute man began to speak. He says, "As they went out, behold, they brought to him a man, mute and demon-possessed. And when the demon was cast out, the mute spoke, and the multitudes marveled, saying, "It was never seen like this in Israel." So the Pharisees are there watching, feeling threatened of course. The Pharisees say, "He cast out demons by the ruler of the demons." Jesus is healing people. Pharisees are going to throw their press-conference twist of lies and fear on it and say, "Oh, well, that healing that you just saw, that's cuz he is the ruler of all demons you know; putting fear into people, not seeing, not witnessing the miracles that are happening right in front of them. They just want to say, "Okay, there's fear in here somewhere. Let's find it. Stir it up, and make people afraid again so that we don't lose any power." Using that to justify furtherance of their need to control. Bible times.

Then, Jesus went about all the cities and villages, teaching in their synagogues, preaching the gospel of the kingdom, and healing every sickness and every disease among the people. But when he saw the multitudes, he was moved with compassion for them, because they were weary and scattered like sheep, having no shepherd. He said to his disciples, "The harvest truly is plentiful, but the laborers are few. Therefore, pray the Lord of the harvest to send out laborers into his harvest." I mean, we're not called to stand by and eat popcorn and watch the football game as the world falls to pieces. We're called to action. We're called to serve, called to help, to bring the word of God, to bring the examples of healing, and to bear testimony of Jesus Christ. We're called to that. We're not called to just watch it all unfold on the television set. He sends out His 12.

John 8 is where Christ is bearing testimony of himself, where they're really holding Him to the fire, trying to get Him to mess up on His answers, and everything He speaks is truth, of course, which makes them even more angry, also of course, but He doesn't back down. He's speaking truth. Let it fall. He's not going to be afraid of somebody threatening Him. The truth doesn't change in the face of threats. He's got to speak the truth. It says in John 10 verse 22 through 30; Now it was the feast of dedication in Jerusalem and it was the winter, and Jesus walked into the temple in Solomon's porch. Then the Jews surrounded him and said to him, "How long do you keep us in doubt? If you are Christ, tell us plainly." You want to know the truth? You want to follow the truth? Follow Jesus and not all of this other buzzy baloney happening in the world. Just follow Jesus. Keep it simple. They're like, "Tell us plainly." Jesus answered them. Listen up. I told you and you do not believe. The works that I do in my Father's name, they bear witness of me. His works are bearing witness to the Father. They're like who? He's just saying, "Pay attention. I told you and you do not believe. The works that I do in my Father's name, they bear witness of me, but you do not believe because you are not of my sheep. As I said to you, my sheep hear my voice and I know them and they follow me." He's saying they follow Him, not some old testament Nebuchadnezzar's gold and insanity. "My sheep hear my voice and I know them and they follow me and I give them eternal life and they shall never perish. Neither shall anyone snatch them out of my hand."

You want to talk about a mama bear; Jesus has got you. You know, when you've got Him in your heart, you're good. You're good. Don't be afraid of some fiery furnace. Even if it really does light you on fire; you're good. You're already good. You're saved. You're done. But you have a mission. You are called to help.

What I just read was saying, "We need to get the word out." Bring that bright light. You're a light on a hill, not sitting in a dark living room watching television. "I give them eternal life, and they shall never perish. Neither shall anyone snatch them out of my hand. My Father who has given them to me is greater than all, and no one is able to snatch them out of my father's hand. I and my father are one." It's kind of like that old schoolyard thing. My dad is bigger than your dad.

I ain't afraid. My dad is bigger than your dad. I ain't going to be spending a bunch of time being scared of something I've seen on the news. Even if it is threatening of my physical safety, you know. It's like what I was talking about tonight with Shadrach, Meshack, and Abednego, thrown in a fiery furnace; Martin Luther King thrown into the Birmingham jail.

Either my last not-a-sermon or the one before that, was about Paul being freed from jail. You know, if you're going to spend your life in faith of Christ, with Christ, Christ in your heart, being afraid if you stand up for truth, you might get thrown in jail, well, honey, there's a lot of examples of which way to go on that one. That ain't a coin flip. You've got tons of examples in the Bible of standing up. You don't have to be afraid. They can threaten you with physical harm or whatever, but you don't need to be afraid. Faith over fear. Faith leads.

Oh, you know what, right after that part that I just read, John 10:22-30 where it says, "My Father who has given them to me is greater than all and no one is able to snatch them out of my Father's hand. I and my Father are one." So, guess what happened just after he said that? Of course, you know what happened next. People started picking up rocks and throwing them. They want to throw rocks at Him because that made them mad. [laughter] Gosh, there's so many examples.

There's one thing I wrote I'll end with this morning. Thinking of Martin Luther King, thinking this "feral" sweatshirt that I'm wearing, and thinking about Jesus all the time. I'm talking about Jesus all the time. I can't stop thinking about Jesus. I wouldn't want to. And I just want to celebrate Jesus all day long, you know. And I was wearing this sweatshirt. It says "feral" on it, and that's like, yeah,

I'm Feral for Jesus. Immago “yeah, you might think I'm a crazy Jesus freak.” There's a great song by Toby Mack and Josiah Queen called “Jesus Freak.” Every time I listen to that song, I get all excited and happy because I'm like, "Yeah, why would I want to do anything other than praise God, celebrate God, help people see the light, help people to find the light, have faith in that light, be solid with each other, move forward, be a beacon on that hill." So, yeah, I'll be feral for Jesus. But anyway, I woke up this morning thinking about Martin Luther King, thinking about Jesus Christ, and I wrote this little thing real quick:

Living proof
right here
where there is
no either/or
of truth
and freedom
with Jesus
always and already
being
everything.

Truth and freedom. Did you read about it? John 8, ye shall know the truth and the truth shall set you free. And he's saying Jesus Christ standing in front of people who are questioning Him, getting more and more upset the more unafraid He is of just speaking plain truth to them.

There is no either/or. It's together. Truth and freedom.

If you're afraid of the truth, you’re not very free. Truth and freedom go together with Jesus. For sure you got Jesus in your heart, by your side, following His light, surrounded with the love of Jesus Christ. Salvation that He paid, for us, that we receive through grace. There's nothing that we could have done to earn such an incredible gift. We're covered, carried with Him, by Him, of Him, for Him, with that grace, with that redemption, with that salvation. You know, truth and freedom are definitely going to go hand-in-hand with Jesus.

All the scary stuff that we see around us is scary; no doubt about it. There's scary stuff happening in the world. But you look and see any politics, or any prejudgments, or any filters, or any but-this but-that but-this but-that but-this but-that but-this but-that but-this but-that.. No. Go ahead and circle the drain all you want or drown in that whirlpool if you want to. You look at a human being, being treated the way we're seeing people treated daily and you ask if you see any injustice. Jesus said, "Even as you have done this to the least of these, my brethren, you have done it unto me."

There was a counter-protest, recently. There's all of these anti-ice protests happening that are just like really just really inspiring and great. So, somebody decided he's going to go show the other side of that. He's going to have a counter-protest, I think 10 or so people showed up for this 'counter-protest'. Most of them scurried away when not more of them showed up. This one counter-protester guy who was left ended up cornered. I don't even know his name. But he ended up being cornered-up against some building while these masses of people were going after him. I mean, non-violence is the way. You cannot kill what is eternal; already eternal. I don't need to go harm somebody else. There's more power, I feel, in saying "why are you doing what you're doing?" I mean, they may kill me dead, my body I mean; that's on the back of anybody's possibilities of either receiving or giving I guess. Non-violence, though.

These throngs of people that are going to go after this one counter-protester guy, who represents everything that they're angry about, everything they've been legit threatened by, everything that's truly messed up about what's going on right now. They see it embodied in this one guy who's come up for a counter-protest with all his hate, and now he's alone; now, they're going to go after him. And he's pressed up against the wall.

Everybody's throwing water balloons at him, snowballs at him, spraying silly string at him, yelling at him, threatening him. He's peeing his pants. He's so scared. Who wouldn't be? I mean, there's all these people that are like, "AHHH!!!" about you. You're the one that all those scary-angry people have in their sights. That'd be scary. Yeah. So, I think he peed his pants. Who wouldn't?

Anyway, there's this one guy, a black guy. I wish that I knew his name. You could search it though; it was somewhere in Minneapolis. I think it happened on January 16th or 17th. I don't know, sometime in these last few days, anyway. He stood up and got between these big angry crowds that wanted to go for this counter-protester guy. It was just like a big chewing machine. It was like an animal-of-a-crowd and this one guy, he got up and blockaded, was a shield to the guy who was probably about to be torn apart. He shielded him. He protected him. Even though, the protector guy being a black guy, is probably somebody that the guy he was protecting had been saying all kinds of terrible stuff about; like, that's all the stuff that he says, all of this racist terrible authoritarian bull crap. But the black guy isn't thinking of that. He's thinking, "This guy's gonna either get seriously harmed or killed. I can't just watch that happen." And he climbed up there, between the big crowd and the scared guy who was being crushed against a building; he protected him, walked him back through the crowd while everybody's still throwing stuff at him, pushing him, punching him, kicking him, yelling at him, all that stuff. And that one guy, a black guy, protected this peed-his-pants-guy that was probably as racist as they can be. Shouldn't say probably. I mean, I don't know. Maybe, maybe not. Everything I hear about him is that he's all the stuff that would not be someone who a person would automatically want to protect. But that one guy just saw a human being in duress, in danger; just like the good Samaritan who helped the Jew who had been beaten up and robbed. You know, the Samaritans and the Jews were not people that sat down and ate bread together. They were not chummy-chummy. They were at odds with each other just by nature of the way the culture had for what they were living at that time. But that good Samaritan, you don't even hear about just a Samaritan, ever. He was such an example for all of us, that Samaritan helping that Jew, that now you just automatically say good Samaritan. Those words go together.

He saw past the person who had been beaten up, beyond faith or culture or differences and said, "There's a human who is broken. I'm going to go help him." and did you know this past weekend is an example of that. You know all the chaos of the world, violence of the world, people being pulled from their houses, people being upset about that, innocent people being shot in the face by their government. Gosh, this is a time; people are raging against that. Standing up against that. Thank God we don’t just sit to the side and eat our popcorn.

This is what Jesus called us to do. We have got we got to shine that light. We need to call that out in a nonviolent way. Going through these times right now, seeing an example of that good Samaritan with that Jew who had been beaten up, assaulted, robbed; that black guy, gosh, I wish I knew his name standing up and protecting that guy who everybody wanted to get at. Everybody wanted to tear at him. He'd said all manner of terrible things about all of them; was there to show them that <u>he</u> was going to be the one that gets to decide all of <u>their</u> fate. Instead, they were going to tear him up; and one guy stood up and said, “Nah.” That's the guy to think about. That's a guy to listen to. That's a guy to say, yeah, he's got the light of Christ in him. That's what Christ wants us to do, to show up for each other. All that other noise is just noise.

Speak plainly. They say in that scripture I just read, they're saying, "You say you're the son of God. Speak plainly. Tell us who are you, the Christ." He says, "You follow my actions. You see what I've done." This was after he done all these miracles. “You see what I've done.” That's the word of God. That is God showing you. That's as plain as it gets. So, you watch for stuff like “Injustice somewhere towards someone is injustice everywhere.” Or ,the guy who is standing in between a frenzied hate mob and a guy who intentionally helped to stir up all that hate, peeing his pants now. Stand in between those two combatants and say, "Hey, let's get you to safety. Let's keep you alive for another day. Let's keep these people from getting your blood on their hands. Show up for that. There's the power of Christ. “You see what I’ve done.”

Following Jesus is what we are called to do. Take off the filters, the blinders, the hatred. King Nebuchadnezzar is wanting us to worship his gold and his power. Whatever form that takes day-by-day; to be afraid of him if we don't, be afraid of him if we say we won't. Simple. Just follow Christ. Follow that light.

Happy Martin Luther King Day. Thank you, God. Thank you, Jesus. I'm your little feral Jesus freak guy. I just keep talking about Jesus. I just want to listen to music about Jesus. Maybe I'll start writing songs about Jesus. Why would I want to talk about anything else? Why would I want to do anything else? Why would I want to follow anyone else? The world goes melting crazy around us. I'm going to keep it simple. I know what to do. Follow Jesus. If you're in fear, look to Jesus. That fear will evaporate.

I'll go where You want me to go, Dear Lord, without fear. I say these things humbly, I promise, following Christ all the way. He has the truth. He knows the truth; the same truth that shall set us all free, in the name of our Lord and Savior Jesus Christ. Amen.

Purple Church of Jesus
greatness
greatness
be what is
for everyone for forever

God's Minneapolis Macramé

February 2, 2026

Welcome to Purple Church of Jesus, where all are welcome, including our dogs, and where all are valuable, necessary, beautiful humans who matter, exactly as we are.

As is our tradition at Purple Church of Jesus, let's start tonight's not-a-sermon with a few moments for meditation, and as a suggested thought, or prompt, to meditate on continuing any sentence that begins with… Jesus.

As my missionary nephew Elder Wilkinson said so perfectly: He allows us to start over Thank God, for all of that. Praise God.
Scripture: Fishers of men
Matthew 4:19
Mark 1:17
Remembering "it is better to teach someone to fish"
Today being groundhog's day, I wrote a poem called:

<u>no shadow</u>
you know when
you have been
Saved by the grace of Jesus
and you cannot hide
the fact that while following
HIM
as HE lives
inside your heart, means
the day will arrive when you won't know
if you still have a shadow.

Comparing what we see in the scriptures to what all of us, or at least most of us, have been seeing in the news this month, whether reading about it or seeing endless videos from ordinary humans like you and I who happened to be at-the-scene-of-these-crimes against our humanity in "real time." What we've been seeing, again and again is real, even as we tell ourselves "I can't believe that this is really happening, right here in our country, to our neighbors, to our friends… to our families; to complete strangers who most of us, without knowing anything about any of their circumstances, can feel within us, and see a desperate need for compassion and protection.

Going back to our meditation at the beginning of tonight's not-a-sermon, meditating on as many different ways we could think of the continuation of a sentence that began with just the name of "Jesus," personally, I can't think of any possible way that any variation a sentence that began with "Jesus" would be reflected in any hand-held video that would be so horrific to watch that I'd have to look away; except for what I'll call "the macramé, or fisherman's net" of humans, showing up with courage, strength, and the power of a thousand cellphones capturing images that even the leaders of a powerful government could not spin into lies and a redirection of blame…

A "Christian" nation, with "values based on the Bible" would not include seeing homes have their front doors busted-in by federalized thugs who then hold the huddled families inside at gunpoint while they pull grandpa outside in the snow in his underwear, under questioning or arrest; who could ever know what he could have possibly done to have warranted that action, taken against him and his family. at the hands of our "Christian nation's" masked-up government, without a warrant; then, returned to his home, with its smashed-in front door, a few hours later after finding that he'd never done anything wrong. No apologies. No offer to repair the damage caused to either this family's home OR their sense of security, at the hands and at the mercy of a country that claims to be "Christian-based…" wanting to strong-arm the whole country into thinking that <u>they're</u> holding onto some special power-Bible that gives them the all of the authority they need over the rest of us; that it's somehow exclusively theirs and with it in hand, they represent the way that everyone should be."

I've gotta say this out loud, as out loud as I could possibly ever say anything that

=MUST - BE - HEARD=

There is NOTHING that Jesus EVER DID, or that He EVER TAUGHT US TO DO that would result in videos - from our streets - the streets of what calls itself "a Christian Nation" - in a world of opposites now sliding unambiguously into "Christian Nationalism" - that would be so dehumanizing, so brutal, so gruesome to see that I'd have to close my eyes; not wanting those images to be imprinted in my brain, in my heart, in my spirit, in my understanding of how easily people can be manipulated, in this "Christian nation" of ours, "One Nation under GOD" into think that shooting a mother in the face as she was trying to drive away, as instructed, from a situation of the government's own instigation, after having broken no laws, whatsoever. Or, an ICU nurse, who gets shoved to the ground as he's trying to help another human, as all nurses are wired to do, who had also just been shoved to the ground in front of him, then being pepper sprayed and SHOT TEN TIMES IN THE BACK while he's already lying on the sidewalk, unarmed, face down… and those who committed these crimes as "federal agents" of "this Christian nation" aka Christian Nationalism, NOT ANYTHING to do with Jesus Christ, or following HIM, just walking away, saying "f'ing b" about the mother they just shot in the face, or actually clapping about the man who they left face down bleeding into the sidewalk, from TEN BULLET HOLES that THEY had JUST FILLED HIM WITH as he was trying to help someone else who had just been pushed to the ground by the same militarized murderers…clapping freely, knowing that those who say that they lead this "Christian Nation" will immediately cover up what we've all seen for ourselves, with piles of mind-bending lies. Just like Jesus…? Be honest.

One Nation Under God and whaddya know, ALL OF IT ABSOLUTELY LIED ABOUT - RIGHT TO OUR FACES - by the "Leaders" of THIS "CHRISTIAN" NATION… and at some point, hopefully, we have got to ask ourselves, honestly, if ANY OF THESE ACTIONS we're ALL SEEING were conducted or led BY representatives of JESUS HIMSELF, or who do we, as "ONE NATION UNDER GOD", HONESTLY THINK that Jesus, standing next to our fellow humans in ANY of those situations, would be raising his fist and saying "YES! Well done my good and faithful servants!", shouting "f'ing B" and clapping as He walked away, thinking "not to worry, the Holy Spirit will just have to go on TV and lie for me later." "One Nation Under God. "Where is JESUS in ANY of those situations. The Land of the Free. One Nation Under God.

In any of these situations, who stands up to defend the Holy Name of Jesus, whose name is, at the very same time, being called out as representing our nation?

<u>Wanting to intentionally remain blind to these facts; blinding others to the same</u>, while collectively praising our Holy Savior, Jesus, who spent his time on earth <u>helping people to see</u>.

Where is Jesus Christ, our true Lord and Savior, in any of that?

If we, as a nation, as a PEOPLE, CANNOT be HONEST about what it truly means and what it truly looks like, to actually be FOLLOWING JESUS, rather than some cultish-level devotion to someone who must be hand delivering the brightest smiles and the biggest guffaws ever heard in hell to the father of lies himself, sitting in a government's highest-high-chair in our current times; at some point ya gotta say c'mon, it's The One or the other, right? And, again honestly, if we as a people who claim to be <u>following Jesus</u>, I've said this before; when people look at us as individuals, or as a country of church congregations that claim be run by principals that are based in "Christianity" we can ask ourselves how any casual observer would answer this same question without immediately knowing the answer; pointing directly at any of those who claim to be Christian, saying
"That's a Christian??"
or
"That's a Christian!!!"

Here's a poem based on the Scripture from Matthew, about not having two masters:

You get one
if it's true…
especially to people who would be upset
for anyone to suggest that the one and
only
Holy Bible
would or could ever
be
anything less than <u>The</u> True Word of God HIMSELF….
then,

Matthew probably meant what he wrote when

Jesus said
no one can serve two masters

so, the most obvious next question
to me, and to
maybe
His true believers who see
would be
who am I always
loved and forgiven by, and who am I
always
having to
prove my love, trust, and devotion to
through looking away.

With the thought still in mind of Matthews written word of what JESUS HIMSELF said about not serving two masters, and going back to the beginning of this not-a-sermon again, in the context of thinking about the TWO GREATEST COMMANDMENTS:

To Love God and
To Love our Neighbor as ourselves.

Then, think about ALL of the extraordinarily brave, ordinary people of Minneapolis, every-day-people just like us, standing up together IN UNITY to help each other, to LOVE THEIR NEIGHBORS no matter whether their skin color matched, their languages were shared, or their perspectives on what was happening in their communities, they just KNEW as HUMANS in a country that pledges allegiance to ONE NATION, UNDER GOD (not under a political party or group of power-hungry politicians - GOD), INDIVISIBLE… with LIBERTY and JUSTICE for

ALL. That is our pledge of allegiance to each other, without party lines OR power lines. Some would call that being a "radical extremist." They used these same types of descriptors as fear-based distractors about Jesus Himself.

I think of the neighbors of Minneapolis all coming together to help each other through the inhumanity we've been seeing through their hundreds, or thousands, of cellphone cameras. Showing us with our own eyes the history that would have been absolutely erased in real-time had they not been there to bear witness. And I think to myself:

We are like God's own macramé; each of us adding our own uncomplicated knots and multicolored beads to what turns out to be that same fishing net that Jesus said to his apostles, "throw your net on the other side of the boat and you will fill your nets with fish, for I will make you fishers of men."

Let's have another moment of meditation to think on those qualities and characteristics of Jesus, and how we can represent HIM in our everyday situations, together, being a part of His macramé, connected-in-representation-and-testimony-of-HIM, our Lord and Savior Jesus Christ, HIS light shining through what we do IN HIS NAME in such a way that ANYONE seeing us as WITNESSES OF HIM, with ALL THAT HE HAS DONE for EACH and EVERY ONE OF US, is in a way that leaves them feeling WAY MORE exclamation points than question marks about who we state that we are following.

…the simple, purposeful beauty of leading people to Jesus by actually following Him.

… two masters? not possible.

Which master's work are we truly seeing?
Which master are we truly following?

Remember to keep it from getting complicated, or from watering the answer down with mealy-mouthed qualifiers, denials, and excuses until arriving at that perfect "spew-thee-out-of-my-mouth" luke-warm temperature….

if you believe in the Bible, and if you believe in Jesus, you get ONE answer.

Here's one more hint: if that ONE ANSWER you get, is one that you're reluctant to SHOUT IT OUT LOUD, to anyone and everyone without qualifications, embarrassment, or shame as "THAT'S THE ONE… The ONE that I choose to follow to the ends of the earth, shouted from the tops of the mountains. The people who are around you, observing you, observing your actions, whether they're complete strangers or not, will show them know for a fact how to answer with one of these two:
That's a Christian??
or
That's a Christian!!

Which of those two versions do you think will lead people to Jesus?

Remember, we are representing HIM and all that He has done without hesitation for us; being honest about who we are reflecting with our actions, and who will or won't be drawn to Him because of what they see us do, and defend. Not only do we get ONE, that One has instructed each of us what is the most important thing we are to do in following him.

Bring people to Him, not to chase them away from Him, even making Him seem repugnant to them, because of what people do to others while professing His name. You get One.

There's this phrase that I love, and that I have had to apply to myself many times, that goes "…painted myself into a corner and stuck-on-stupid again."

Standing there like that, realizing after the fact that I've got a choice to make. Ego-based option being: stand there and wait for the paint to dry, not asking for help, or being too embarrassed to tell anyone about having that "human moment", or, as we hear all-the-dang-time now, "doubling down" by pretending it never happened, walking straight across that still-wet-paint, grabbing another fresh can, and painting ourselves back into the same dang corner again-and-again, saying "I meant to do that!" "This is the way it's supposed to be done! If you disagree with me doing it this way then you're a radical extremist, and…oh yeah… everybody say rah-rah-rah for doing it this way!"

Or, as my missionary nephew, so beautifully, and so perfectly said at Christmas time, as we were remembering and celebrating the Birth of Christ, "Jesus made the way for us to be able to start again."

You get ONE.

Choose Wisely.

Personally, trying to remember and reflect the same words that I end each of my not-a-sermons with, and each of my prayers; as I move through each day, with each of my actions and my interactions with others who are sharing this same planet, this path, this journey through life… with what I carry of myself through each of these moments; words, behaviors, and actions followed with exclamation marks, rather than question marks, saying "in the name of Jesus Christ, amen."

Jesus Christ gave me everything and asked ONLY that I follow him. As I try my best to show my respect and love for Him, and all that He has done for me, rather than seeing more of our state-of-dysfunction-disunion-destruction…

…it is the healing light of JESUS that I'm hoping people will see, being drawn to Him, so that maybe they too will be able to feel what I have found to be incredible.

You get ONE.
Whose holy macramé are we going to choose, whose fishing net, whose faces will light up alongside ours as they see the that SAME BRIGHT LIGHT from the Top of the Hill that has changed OUR lives, by lighting us up too.

Then, if you're feeling extra brave about taking it to the next level, from the chapter in Matthew immediately before the one about not being able to serve two masters, we have, Matthew Chapter 5 verses 43-48.

Praise God, we get to have As Many Resets as we need, up to and including our very last day on earth, "the last shall be first" after all, even if we're still stuck on that painted-in-corner for a while, Jesus will be right there with us, saying "Please, with all of my love, as you decide on which one to choose…

choose Me."

Thank God, for all of that. Praise God.

I say all of these things, with my genuine heart, in the name of my Lord and Savior Jesus Christ, amen.

Purple Church of Jesus

greatness

greatness

be what is

♡ for everyone for forever ♡

Black History Month 2026
February 26, 2026

All right. Welcome to Purple Church of Jesus. There you go, Mr. AppleJacks. Yeah, where we all are welcome, all are needed,
all are beautiful and worthy and loved just as we are. Most of all, all of our dogs, too. What you got there? Little sticker there. Okay, so let's do this. I was working on new poems that I didn't finish yet, but that is not the title of our not sermon today. Apple Jack's helped me write it. You wanted me to know what was important to write about. So, we're going to have moment of meditation first like we do, AppleJacks. All right

I'm working on a poem called "one not done." You know that phrase "one-and-done." It's based on that, like, do one and you're done. It's like a play on words but, let me get a little pillow here. Come on. Yeah. One for me and one for my AppleJacks. Here you go buddy. Do you want a pillow or is that going to be uncomfortable?

Okay. So, yeah; One, semicolon, not done. Like, okay, you won, but that ain't mean you're done. That's what it's about.

I wanted to start tonight's not a sermon by reading from Matthew 25 verses 14-30. Matthew 25. You want to read this one, buddy? verses 14-30. Here we go. Here's a little story for you. Little story from Jesus. Okay. Matthew 25:14-30. The parable of the talents.

For the kingdom of heaven is like a man traveling to a far country who called his own servants and delivered his goods to them. And to one he gave five talents, to another two, and to another one, to each according to his own ability. Didn't give him more than he could carry. And

immediately he went on a journey. Then he who had received the five talents went and traded with them and made another five talents.
And likewise, he who had received two gained two more. Where did I go? Yeah, gained two more also. But he who had received one went and dug in the ground and hid his lord's money. After a long time, the lord of those servants came and settled accounts with them.

Buddy, we got a few more to go. Let's see, turn in the page with a little bit of help from my buddy. So, when he who had received five talents came and brought five other talents, saying, "Lord, he delivered to me five talents. Look, I have gained five more talents besides them." His lord said to him, "Well done, good and faithful servant. You were faithful over a few things. I will make you ruler over many things. enter into the joy of your Lord. He who had received two talents came and said, "Lord, you delivered to me two talents. Look, I have gained two more talents besides them." His lord said to him, "Well done, good and faithful servant. You have been faithful over a few things. I will make you ruler over many things. Enter into the joy of your Lord." Then he who had received the one talent came and said, "Lord, I knew you to be a hard man reaping where you have not sown and gathering where you have not scattered seed. And I was afraid and went and hid your talent in the ground. Look there, you have what is yours, still sitting in there in the ground." But his lord answered and said to him, "You wicked and lazy servant, you knew that I reap where I have not sown and gather where I have not scattered seed. So you ought to have deposited my money with the bankers. And at my coming I would have received back my own with interest."

So, take the talent from him and give it to him who has 10 talents because he's doing stuff with his even though he already has a lot. For to everyone who has more will be given, and he will have abundance. But from him who does not have, even what he has will be taken away. And cast the unprofitable servant into outer darkness. There will be weeping and gnashing of teeth.

We're talking about talents, magnifying our talents; parable of the talents. You know, I should magnify dogs. I should just have lots of dogs. Hi, AppleJacks. it's you and me. The parable of talents, specifically with the direction of multiplying our talents versus burying them and saving them for later, is a parable that I'll bet a lot of people who have spent time reading the Bible and listening to stories about the parables of Jesus are already familiar with.

Remember, he said this is like the kingdom of heaven. That's how he started it. I remember hearing this same parable of the talents from that time when I was a little kid going to Sunday school. But from then until now, I had always thought of a talent being purely about what of ourselves we have been given in character and abilities and heart that we are able to bring forward and multiply. And it is about that, really. But I have also wondered about the burying part of the story with the person who had been given one talent.

Of course, it's easily understood as being one who doesn't develop their talents, who doesn't shine their light for people to see and testify of Jesus Christ, whether by example or by words, but is also, back in those Bible times, a measurement of physical weight. So, I looked it up and found that a talent was the largest unit of weight in the ancient world, measuring-in at the equivalent of what we would measure as approximately 75 to 76 pounds today; maybe you didn't know that either. I didn't know it until I looked it up. Thinking of it that way, imagine the heft of carrying five talents or 375 pounds, multiplied by the time their master returned, to 750 pounds. Or, two talents being 150 pounds multiplied to 300 pounds, or one talent only 75 pounds, just buried for later.

Those were the weights that they used to measure gold or silver; stuff like that. For some reason, for me at least, thinking of these talents with this method of measuring resonates a little bit more. Don't get me wrong, thinking of magnifying our talents also relates to talents as we use the word now. At least I think of it that way, like, I can sometimes sort of try to play the banjo and through practicing a whole lot can someday play, maybe the super-duper-banjo great way, or who knows, I could magnify my talents even further by learning to play a fiddle or a harmonica or a whole drum kit and sing all at the same time all for Jesus. That would be fantastic. I'd be praising God through music everywhere that I went. I still want to do that. Hopefully more people will be drawn to Him than repelled. Hah! What is that noise?

Reading further from Matthew 25, remembering that early in this same chapter that we read from during the last month's not a sermon, Jesus has spent the first few verses pouring out heaping levels of scorn on… which group was it again? Not any of our country's current favorite pastime of "name-your-minority-community with a clever, stinging slur" I'm sure. His scorn over and over again was saved for who?

The hypocrites.

For some reason, in our "Christian nation"… you hear people like to call this is a "Christian nation". Christian nationalism is not at all Christian. Know the difference between those two. They'll try to pass one off as the other.

Pay attention. They're polar opposites. It's like, Satan's half-lie version of Christianity.

You know how he would like tell some truth, and then throw in a lie, sometimes a great big lie, and make the make the lie more palatable by putting a little bit of truth around it. Imagine putting a poison pill into a little sugary treat, or healthy treat, like “Hey, that looks good!” Who was it? Snow White with the poison apple. “Hey that apple looks good!”

That also fits well with the Bible’s apple thing. You get the point. Christian nationalism is like Satan's version of calling this “a Christian nation” or claiming “being Christian” while on a spirit-grift; period. Not the same thing as what Jesus Christ taught by word <u>and example</u> throughout His life. For some reason, in our “Christian nation,” there are still gobs and gobs of slurs to choose from. We never run out of them. Which flavor will it be today? Any of the racist variations about people of color or another sexual orientation; you know what it seems like we do run out of? Love.

Hate juggles like a nod-and-wink hot potato thrown into the air for long enough to capture our nation's attention, then, deny it all, pleading absolute innocence while your fingers cool back off again through our country’s teeny-tiny attention span. Sound familiar? If it doesn't, you're not paying attention, intentionally or not, while people are routinely called “illegals” without any embarrassment or shame; as if “illegals” is even a word. Colonizer’s English, after all, being important to speak correctly, at least by people who say it's our nation's “official language.” Use it correctly if you want to say it's our official language. “Illegals.” Really; it's not a word. English teachers can tell you at the starting point of middle school that illegals is not a noun. It's just a made up hate-word; plain old code for that same old dehumanizing racism. Just like the anti-LGBTQIA+ or DEI hate-words for "everything-other" dot-dot-dot; fill in your own blanks.

Let's read Matthew 25, in that same chapter verses 35 and 40. For I was hungry. This is all red letter. This is all Jesus talking. For I was hungry and you gave me food. I was thirsty and you gave me drink. I was a stranger and you took me in. I was naked and you clothed me. I was sick and you visited me. I was in prison and you came to me.

This is what a Christian nation would be doing by following Christ. I was in prison and you came to me. Then the righteous will answer him saying, Lord, when did we see you hungry and feed you or thirsty and give you drink? When did we see you a stranger and take you in or naked and clothe you? Or when did we see you sick or in prison and come to you? And the king will answer and say to them, "Assuredly I say to you, in as much as you did it to one of the least of these, my brethren, you did it to me."

You know, I can't help but think while reading that set of verses, why is it controversial to release the complete Epstein files? Why is that a difficult case to prosecute; or to even bring any charges?

…as much as ye have done it to the least of these, my brethren, ye have done it to me.

I mean, that's not even going to begin addressing where he was with how you are to treat children. What happens to people who abuse them, who lead them away from him? You know, this Christian nation sure has a complicated time trying to figure out what to do about pedophiles that have billions of dollars and have lots of power. Suddenly, it's more complex. Suddenly, we have little conflict of interest. Yes, conflict of conscious; a conflict of conscience for sure.

In this "Christian nation" where Jesus spells out clearly, I don't know how much more clear you could be about right and wrong when it comes to child sex trafficking, period. Throw in that it's a bunch of billionaires and power brokers tossing kids back and forth like pawns. Come on.
I got off track, but golly, there's so much B.S. going on with this "Christian nation" right now, with everything being exhaustively buried beneath tons-and-tons of "what-about-isms."

"Christian nationalism" has nothing to do with "Christian Christianity." "…as much as ye have done it unto the least of these, my brethren, ye have done it unto me." Thinking about that in the light of how we treat minorities in our country; how we treat trafficked minorities in our country. It's interesting to me how hatred and slurs still proliferate so easily in our Christian nation where we so frequently refer to the very same Bible where Jesus gave so much emphasis to calling out the hypocrites. In fact, he devoted exactly 0% of the time that he spent during his three whole years of holy-bandwidth on what we now have firmly in place as our "Christian nation's"somehow politely-palatable phrase "DEI." Tell me that DEI has anything to do with Jesus Christ and I will immediately call BS.

February, in case you don't already know, is Black History Month. The guvment-ficials in D.C. ain't talking about it too much, are they, cuz that would mean looking at the humanity that is to be ignored or disposed of under the newly invented terms-of-recognition represented by these three grossly misused letters; meaning that you have "official permission" to leave your head wedged way up your behind about anything that isn't primarily or exclusively flavored with white-entitlement "DEI."

In the very same month that we still don't have to look very far. or look for it at all really, to see and smell the stink of racism; speech-pollution being spewed from what calls itself the highest office in the land; always presenting such a fine example of Christ for our deeply-cult-level-devotion to His opposite.

Bringing this to Jesus, and to his parable of magnifying and multiplying our talents; in light of Black History Month, the heavy lifting that the weight of the talents refer to, and the responsibility associated with magnifying that, hear this about the true hero of a man named Megar Evers and his true hero wife Myrlie.

Reading this directly from African-American history, this is probably banned and dismissed as DEI; while we see history being erased and re-written in real time. But not this one. I'm gonna put it right in the middle of my not-a-sermon to last one more place for forever. Reading from AfricanAmerican History Forever about Medgar Evers and his wife Mrylie Evers:

Her babies were on the floor when the shot rang out. By the time she reached the driveway, history had changed forever. Just after midnight on June 12th, 1963.

By the way, I was already during alive at this time. It's not as long ago as you'd think that it something like this would be. Although, honestly, we are still seeing parallels to this story in our nation's history continue to happen today. To continue the story of Medgar and Myrlie Evers:

Just after midnight on June 12th, 1963, Medgar Evers pulled into his driveway in Jackson, Mississippi. He had spent the day organizing, investing, investigating racial violence, pushing for voter registration. Power pushing for voter registration in a state where being black and bold could get you killed. He stepped out of his car holding a bundle of t-shirts printed with the words Jim Crow must go. He never made it inside. A single sniper's bullet tore through his back. Inside the house, his children, trained by their father in the rituals of survival, dropped to the floor at the sound of gunfire. They already knew what to do. And then Myrlie Evers Williams opened the door. What she saw, no wife should ever have to see. Her husband bleeding into the Mississippi night. Her partner in struggle, the father of her three children. He died at a hospital that initially hesitated to treat him because he was black.

This was in 1963 Mississippi. He was 37 years old. How many people do you know, yourself included, me included, could come even close to what this superhero did by the time he was 37? Not very many, not me. He was only 37 years old. But this story is not only about the bullet. It's about what came after. Mississippi in 1963, a state at war with its own citizens. Gosh, does that sound like anything you would recognize today? It does to me; loud and clear.

Medgar Evers was the NAACP's first field secretary in Mississippi. That title sounds administrative. It was not. He investigated lynchings.

You aren't going to find that in our history books anymore, after DEI erases everything. He investigated lynchings. Those happened.
No matter how much they want to erase that fact, that is the history of our country.

He documented beatings. He pushed to integrate the University of Mississippi. He organized boycotts He trained young activists. Mississippi was the stronghold of white supremacy.

Think there's any more of that? Be honest, Christian nation.

Mississippi was the stronghold of white supremacy. The White Citizens Council operated in suits instead of hoods, but its mission was the same. Preserve segregation by any means necessary. The murder weapon traced quickly to Byron Dea Beckwith, a member of that council. The evidence was clear. Justice was not surprised.

Just ICE... Justice. Two different things.

At the first trial, the district attorney openly asked potential jurors whether they believed killing a black man in Mississippi was a crime.
Let that settle. He's asking the jurors, "Do you even, I mean, let's establish a baseline here. Do you think it it's a crime to kill a black man?" That had to be a question. Seven black men appeared in the jury pool and none were seated. Pretend you're surprised. The all-white, all male jury deadlocked. The sitting governor, Ross Barnett, publicly shook the defendant's hand in the courtroom. 1963. Same today. They would just do it behind doors. A second trial ended the same way. A third was quietly abandoned. Beckwith walked free. Even though all the evidence was there and he was guilty, the state had answered its own question.

Kind of like you see now with ICE; just five seconds after somebody gets murdered by them, they're like, "Oh, well that was because that person was a this-or-that or a this-or-that-Assassin-terrorist, you know. They're going to do their own investigation, their own internal investigation, and… what do you know? Nobody's ever convicted. Nobody's ever found guilty of anything." Pretend that you're surprised.

The state had answered its own question just like today. grief as resistance. Many people would have folded under that weight. Myrlie did not. His wife, she was 30 years old. Thirty. Only Thirty. Raising three children alone in a nation that had just watched her husband die on television. She left Mississippi for safety. But she did not leave the fight. She ran for Congress. She spoke across the country. She guarded Medgar's memory like sacred fire. Still is. Civil rights movement did not pause after 1963. It accelerated. That same year, the Birmingham campaign exposed police dogs and fire hoses turned on children.

This is a Christian nation. How far do you think we've come from there? Come on. Honesty counts.

The March on Washington echoed with I have a dream. Four little girls were killed in the 16th Street Baptist Church bombing. That was all in that same year. The nation was convulsing. In 1964, the Civil Rights Act passed. In 1965, after the blood of Selma stained the Edmund Pettis Bridge, the Voting Rights Act became law, which since that time, politicians have done nothing but try to water it back down, get rid of it.

Women had to fight for their right to vote, too. That's a whole another story. Why is it that when power feels threatened it does such bull-shitty things? By following Jesus Christ's version of Christianity? Be honest. Ask the Native Americans about the smallpox-infested blankets that they were given, Christian nation.

So, in 1964, the Civil Rights Act passed. And in 1965, after the blood of Selma stained the Edmund Pettis Bridge, the Voting Rights Act became the law. But Medgar Evers killer still slept in his own bed. Myrlie Evers kept asking why; thirty-one years. But in 1989, investigative journalist Jerry Mitchell uncovered something chilling. The Mississippi Sovereignty Commission, a state agency created to undermine civil rights. Let that sink in. A state agency created to undermine civil rights.

Does that exist today?

These leaders had secretly assisted in shaping the original juries.

Go figure. Look at anything from the DOJ regarding the Epstein files today. Oh, there's nothing shady going on there. You get nothing but straight answers and honesty from the head of the DOJ. Yeah, nothing but truth and standing up for the people of our country against crime. It's so full of nonsense and B.S.

The trials had not merely failed. They had been engineered. This is back in 1989, 31 years later. Myrlie took that truth and refused to let it go to dust. This is the truth of the state agency that had been created to undermine civil rights leaders which had been secretly assisting in shaping the original juries. So Medgar Evers' wife took that truth and refused to let it gather dust. She pushed prosecutors. She knocked on doors. She invoked her husband's name like a summons. In 1994, 31 years after that midnight shot, Byron de la Beckwith was tried again; in 1994. This time the jury was integrated, scandalous all by itself. This time the machinery of Mississippi bent toward truth. That was a hard bend toward truth. He was convicted of murder and sentenced to life in prison. And he died behind bars in 2001.

Less than 10 years in jail, died there after 31 years from the time that he murdered Medgar Evers and got away with it. He died behind bars in 2001. Think about what it means to carry grief that long. Never let it turn into surrender.

The arc of her life. Myrlie Evers later became chairwoman of the NAACP. NAACP. The very organization her husband served. In 2013, she delivered the invocation of President Barack Obama's second inauguration. the first woman and first lay person ever to do so. Fifty years after kneeling beside her dying husband, she stood at the Capitol and prayed over a nation. That's not a coincidence. That is the long arc of black struggle. Reconstruction betrayed to Jim Crow enforced to Freedom Riders beaten, Medgar Evers shot in his driveway, and still the movement pressed forward. Because black history is not just the story of what was taken. Its the story of who refused to let the taking be the final word.

What she did next. Myrlie Evers did not allow her husband's murder to become a closed chapter. She turned private devastation into public demand. She taught her children that their father's life mattered.
She taught Mississippi that time would not erase accountability.
And she taught America that justice delayed can still be claimed if someone refuses to stop knocking. Her strength was not loud. It was enduring. And endurance in the black freedom struggle has always been revolutionary. Her children were crawling on the floor when the shot rang out. But their mother stood up. She never sat down until justice did.

That is just the best, and I give all of the credit for that whole story that appeared on African-American history. So, look that up. African-American history. This is Black History Month. There's a million stories that you probably have access to if you haven't seen or heard anyone talking about Black History Month. Do some research. Look it up.

That's the greatness that I love. I recently found a great t-shirt that says, "Never argue with somebody John Brown would have shot." So great. If you are someone like me, who, until a few years ago went all the way through school and life so far without even knowing that there was an anti-racist guy back then named John Brown. I suggest that you look him up and do some homework like I finally did, and ask yourself "why didn't they tell me about this guy while I was in school?"

When I began this kind-of-sermony not-a-sermon by quoting from Matthew about multiplying our talents, rather than burying them, and then the heavy lifting that referring to talents really implied back in those Bible times. I'm hoping to convey that our work here is not done.

Honoring Black History Month; honor it. Honor the people that deserve to be honored, and all of our thanks for being brave enough to be honorable. Medgar Evers knew that the heavy lifting he was doing in this "Christian nation" would likely result in him being murdered. What you do? What do you do if you're his young widow, raising their small children; wanting to find justice for your husband. It took until 1994, from 1963, for his murderer, known murderer, to go to prison.

Justice, justice for all or Just-ICE. You get One. Who do you follow? You get one.

Don't be afraid to do that heavy lifting of being honorable, of doing your part to bring about the hard bend of history to justice.

Black History Month. Pay attention to it. Learn about it. Learn about some of your own heroes who you don’t even know about yet. And, if you're a whitey like me, wait, was that a slur I just called myself? Maybe it doesn't count since I'm white; and you don't know who John Brown is, look him up. See if you can find any lessons to learn about him and the life that he bravely lived. Black History Month. Nobody gets to erase it.

I say all of these things humbly and meaningfully, in the name of our Lord and Savior Jesus Christ. Amen.

Purple Church of Jesus

greatness

greatness

be
what
is

♡ for everyone for forever ♡

Faith Already Knows to Just Keep On Moving Mountains

Faith Already Knows to Just Keep-On Moving Mountains

March 12, 2026

Hello. Here I am with Apple Jacks. And we're having a little open mic day today. Mr. Applejacks. sound good? That's cool. This is our little spot. Yes. Right. My friend Apple and me, he's a good boy. Just wanted to do a quick check-in for open mic night. See, we have open mic on the second; every second matters. So, it's every second Thursday of the month. And not-a-sermons are every last Thursday because the last shall be first. So, today is the second Thursday of the month. Apple Jacks and I are here to have open mic.

I just wanted to do a quick check in and say, guess what? It's March of 2026, which means that… what do you see over there AppleJacks?

This being the month of the one-year anniversary of Purple Church of Jesus, my Apple Jacks seeing something, I got this tattoo. Let's see if you can see it. It's a unicorn right next to the last shall be first. Halo'd J, on the first day of our very first not-a-sermon. I don't know if you can see it. I got that purple unicorn cuz of course, how could you not have a purple unicorn tattoo? And then the date, it's probably backwards because the way I'm filming this, but uh 3 27 25, that was our very first Purple Church of Jesus; very first not-a-sermon. I got lots of flack for swearing so much in that one. And that's okay cuz it was making a point.

And then, look around here. Let's see if I can get to it. I don't know if you can. There we go; kind of wonder if I go like this. There's a praying mantis. That's Jesus in the Garden of Gethsemane paying for our sins, bleeding from every pore. There's my walking stick bug. That is representative of me. I used to be a regular stick, then somehow, 'cuz of you-know-who, I was able to become a walking stick bug and move from place to place instead of just being stuck. A stick that was broken off; now I'm a walking stick bug because of Jesus. And then if I can get way over here, there you go. All the bugs. So, there's Jesus in Gethsemane, the walking stick bug, but where is the walking stick bug going? He's following the Holy Spirit; little mister Firefly lighting the way. So, pretty cool that I got all these together. The last shall be first. My Halo'd J, purple unicorn, of course celebrating the very first day of Purple Church of Jesus.

So, just wanted to check in and say hi, most importantly, JESUS SAVES; (my throat tattoo, gotten the day before being re-baptized, so it went into the water with me).

…the thing about faith moving mountains, my little realization for today, cuz I learn just a little bit at a time. I'm not too good at learning it all at once. It's probably better that way, but I learn a little bit at a time. And the thing about faith moving mountains has been on my mind, how I have experienced a miracle, a true miracle, December the 6th of 2025, that I had not seen coming. It was brought to me through the blood of Jesus, being baptized, Saved, receiving the gift of the Holy Spirit on December the 6th, 2025. So, I'm just having this amazing miracle, this amazing experience that hasn't left me. But then, you know, you've got, you got to feed your faith. I haven't lost faith. No. And maybe it's a natural thing that this is not at the crescendo level that it was when I got baptized and saved and received the Holy Spirit. Maybe that's normal; sustaining faith is not a one and done. It isn't like, okay, there's the trumpets playing, there's arms of Jesus hugging me, loving me. exactly as I am, paying for

my sins, the grace of God, bringing me salvation. All of that is secure. All of that is true and all of that is known by me and has not changed since that day.
But it ain't a one and done, man.

I'm hearing those trumpets; it's a beautiful sound. Feeling all that joy is a beautiful feeling. Raising my hands up to God like a little kid saying, "Hey, pick me up. He's got me." Gosh, it's so beautiful. Sustaining this, I didn't think that, okay, it's automatic. I've got to put in the work, you know; the faith will move mountains. It was not a "one mountain" thing. There's more to go. God's welcomed me in his arms. Jesus paid the price for me to be here. That does not mean "all right. You just sit over there and we'll play bingo for the rest of eternity." We've got work to do.

Faith will move mountains. One moved. It did. Anybody that knows me can tell you it did. My wife still tells me, she says, "You've changed." I say, "Yeah." They don't call this 'born again' for nothin". That's real. I have, you know, and then what's next?

Not knowing what's next does not equal done. Showing up and asking God, "What do you need me to do today? Help me to understand what the world is doing today. Help me to understand my place in the world and who I need to see and talk to, who I need to listen to, where I need to go next, what I need to do. I'm here for you, God. And that faith, the same faith that brought me to the miracle of my baptism and receiving the Holy Spirit, being saved on December the 6, 2025; the one-year-this-month anniversary of Purple Church of Jesus being born… that it exists at all is a miracle itself.

What has happened to me since that time is a miracle for sure. But that does not mean that those are the only mountains that are going to move with faith and showing up with my puppy AppleJacks.

What are you doing over there, friend? You taking a little nap? We're going to finish our walk out here at our outdoor church; this is our other sanctuary.

We're going to go have some fun, but I wanted to check in. It's open mic night, which I don't record. And yeah, I mean, people need to have a place to speak their truths without thinking, 'well, you know, is this going to end up on YouTube with the not-a-sermons, or somebody's going to be writing all this down somehow and, you know, people need to have their safe space and not have to worry about what anybody else is going to say or think about it. It could be just open ink pen; nobody has to even say anything out loud in order to sit there and be in a safe place with people who understand you, love you, are there for you no matter what and we all just write together. You matter. You're beautiful. You're important. You have something to bring to this world that nobody else can. So, show up for that. Show up for all that.

That's what I keep doing, trying to keeping the faith for, cuz that's the faith. That's the faith that'll move mountains… plural. I'm glad you're here with me. Peace and love. Happy one-year month for Purple Church of Jesus all the way there. The last shall be first. Thank you, Jesus.

Over here. Yeah, you're going to see him again. There you go. There you go. I think I don't know how to hold the camera. There you go. There's my Jesus Garden of Gethsemane praying mantis tattoo turning a regular broken-off stick into a walking stick again with the direction of following the Holy Spirit, mister Firefly. All right. Peace and love. I'll talk to you soon; ain't going nowhere. I'm going act in faith because I don't know where is next. But my faith will tell me I'm going to keep that intact. Happy March. Happy almost one year, Purple Church of Jesus. We'll be doing the not-a-sermon on the last Thursday of this month, like we do every last Thursday, and it'll be the one-year mark

If I didn't already say it, I love you. And I say these things in this beautiful place with my beautiful dog who is taking a little nap. Say hello, Mr. AppleJacks. Can you say hi? And then we're gonna go. We're gonna go play some more. Yeah, that's my buddy. That's my good boy, AppleJacks, say it with me... in the name of Jesus Christ Hallelujah. for dogs, amen.

Purple Church of Jesus

greatness

greatness

be
what
is

♡ for everyone for forever ♡

Letting Go; also, Never Letting Go

Letting Go; also, Never Letting Go
March 25, 2026

All right, this is it. This is our Purple Church of Jesus moment. We'll probably stop these now. There's enough on there already. It's kind of tough to keep it going cuz it takes a lot out of me, but Jesus has got it. I've recorded enough of them to say what's up with what. At least as far as I can see things. And my AppleJacks and I… He's been running around; that's why he's breathing so hard. We're having fun at our spot. What's that? What is it? What was that over there?

You know, watch any of those other Purple Church of Jesus videos if you want to, or don't, because we're going to keep on finding our joy, AppleJacks. Yeah, I'll keep the physical Purple Church of Jesus space for probably another year anyway. My phone number is on stuff where there's a way to get a hold of me if you want to go over there and hang out. I'll be around. I ain't going nowhere. Jesus has got me. I ain't letting go of Jesus. He's not letting go of me neither. AppleJacks and I are going to keep on doing our thing. That's right. You ready to go play, bud? Let's go. Peace and love y'all. We made it one year. All the stuff I needed to say is there. I'll write another book; Jesus Saves. Whoever's gonna find him is gonna find him and he's going to find them regardless of what I say or how I go about it. I wish that if I could say one thing, it would be that Christian churches have got to stop doing what they do to LGBTQ people cuz that sucks. It's abuse; spiritual abuse. So, if you're a unicorn like me who didn't make it onto Noah's ark, cuz there was not going to be a place for us in the world anyway, if you feel like that, ever, know that you've got a place with Jesus and with Apple Jacks and me. We're going to always be around, especially Jesus. So, don't let go of that; right, AppleJacks. Should we go play? Let's go run around and do some more fun. Peace and love y'all forever in the name of Jesus Christ, amen.

Purple Church of Jesus

greatness

greatness

be what is

♡ for everyone for forever ♡

Remembering the Potter’s Field

Remembering the Potter’s Field
April 3, 2026

…guess we're starting with a meditation.

It's Good Friday today, so you need something to meditate about. Maybe think about Good Friday. pastor toddymanners here with Purple Church of Jesus, in Purple Church of Jesus. And I wasn't sure I was going to be doing any more of these, but you know, if there's ever a time…

…a friend of mine used to tell me, he's passed away now, but I'll never forget what he would tell me. He'd say, "Todd, get over your cheap self” when I got too in my problems, too in my head, too in my worries, too in my whatever. He'd tell me, "Get over your cheap self." And at first I'd get upset like, "What are you telling me that for? My stuff is real, you know? I got… I got stuff I'm working on. I got problems, man. I got problems. I got reasons for the way I am. You ain't seen the trouble I've seen, you know.” He'd say, "Todd, get over your cheap self. You think you're the only one who’s got stuff?”

I’d needed to hear that, you know. Thank God for him. He probably saved my life. But, if there was ever a time for any of us to get over our cheap selves, it would be on Good Friday; today. You think about Good Friday next time you're thinking about how big your troubles are. You think about Jesus on Good Friday. That's a good place to start our meditation for today.

I've been really hung up; I've been depressed as you can imagine, well maybe not but I mean everybody around me is like “what's going on Todd?” Everybody. It's like, I don't

know. It's been… it's been a rough couple weeks. I got good people around me. I got Jesus here with me in my heart, you know, and it just… sometimes gets pretty dark in there. And Jesus has got that light shining and I ain't going to drop out of life even when I'm really sad because I got that light in my heart. You know, Jesus has got me. And, you know, I was thinking I wasn't going to be doing any more of these. You know, if there's ever a time for me to get over my cheap self, at least for a day, at least for a minute, maybe a moment, long enough to remember Good Friday. So, here we are.
Good Friday.

I'm going to start by reading from Matthew chapter 27. Jesus is handed over to Pilate. This is the New King James Version of the Bible. Greatness. Matthew Chapter 27 verse one, on Good Friday. When morning came, all the chief priests and elders of the people plotted against Jesus to put him to death. When he had bound… when they had bound him, led him away and delivered him to Pontius Pilate the governor. Then Judas, his betrayer, seeing that he had been condemned, was remorseful and brought back the 30 pieces of silver to the chief priests and elders, saying, "I have sinned by betraying innocent blood." And they said, "What is that to us? You see to it." Then he threw down the pieces of silver in the temple and departed and went and hanged himself.

Remember that part where the last shall be first. Remember; remember that part. Okay.

So there goes Judas confessing his sins, throwing the silver down, them saying, "What is that to us?" And then he goes and hangs himself. The chief priests took the silver pieces and said, "It is not lawful to put them into the treasury because they are the price of blood." And they consulted together and bought with them the potter's field to bury strangers in. Therefore, that field has been called the field of blood to this day. Then was fulfilled what was spoken by Jeremiah the prophet, saying, "And they took the 30 pieces of silver, the value of"… this is… you know, they call it Good Friday, but it's hard to read this part of the Bible. They took the 30 pieces of… okay, get it together. They took the 30 pieces of silver, the value of Him who is priced, whom they of the children of Israel priced, and gave them for the potter's field as the Lord directed me.

I'm going to read the that part again because I kind of lost it there for a minute. So again, Matthew 27, I'm going to start at verse six.

But the chief priests took the silver pieces and said, "It is not lawful to put them into the treasury because they are the price of blood." And they consulted together and bought with them the potter's field to bury strangers in. Therefore, that field has been called the field of blood to this day. Then this is now verse nine. Then was fulfilled what was spoken by Jeremiah the prophet, saying, "And they took the 30 pieces of
Silver, the value of him who was priced, whom they of the children of Israel priced, and gave them for the potter's field as the Lord directed me." that last part; as the Lord directed me.

You know, we all know what happened. We all know the story of Judas betraying Jesus with a kiss, you know, getting paid 30 pieces of silver, hanging himself and being buried in that potter's field. We know this story. And, as I was reading it, what jumped out at me said, "And they consulted together and bought with them the potter's field to bury strangers in." Where in the Bible are you hearing about strangers? Where do you remember hearing anything about strangers? Just a couple chapters before that, you get the very famous verses from Matthew chapter 25. I'm going to start at verse 31 in chapter 25. And this is all in red letters, so this is all Jesus talking. Matthew 25:31 starting there. When the Son of Man comes in his glory and all the holy angels with him, then he will sit on the throne of his glory. And the nations will be gathered before him, and he will separate them one from the other as a sheep herd divides his sheep from the goats. And he will set the sheep on his right hand and the goats on the left.

You know, I used to, I still kind of do, I'm like, "Well, okay, the sheep and the goats and like the goats are… it's implied that the goats are like, the not the good ones, you know." And I'm like, "Well, goats are pretty cool. I love goats. Goats are awesome. You know, they do that baby goat yoga stuff and they're just so cute. Goats are so cool. I love goats." And I'm thinking, "Why are they… why do they keep calling goats in the Bible like that, like it's not a good thing, because goats are really cool." But then, as I was reading it this time, when I was thinking of goats again, I'm thinking there's that part where the you know it's the sheep are the good ones, on the right side, and the goats… separating the sheep from the goats. And then I thought of that phrase that we've got in whatever modern culture; it's probably, I mean, I'm an old guy so this has probably been around forever and I just don't… takes me a while sometimes to figure out what the cool stuff is. But a "GOAT" being like "Greatest Of All Time." And so, I thought of goats like that. Like the "greatest of all time" being an ego thing. Like "oh, I'm the greatest of all time. I'm a goat!" and ego being something that separates us from God. Separates us from Jesus Christ. Separates us from submitting our will to Jesus Christ because, "hey, I've got it. I'm I'm a goat!" Not a cute little goat, obviously, but you know what I mean? The greatest of all time! I'm, Yeah,

I'm the I'm the one, or I'm like, "Yeah, I can do this all by myself! I'm the greatest! I'm the greatest of all time!" and that ego getting in the way of the grace. Well, not the grace; the grace has got us no matter what. No matter how long it takes us to get through however we learn and progress in Christ, the grace of Jesus Christ has got us, even if we're full of ourselves, but separating me from being able to be effective in the way that Christ needs me to be, that gets impaired or impeded or however you want to put it if I'm full of myself, if I haven't been able to figure out how to get over my cheap self for long enough to be grateful for the price that Jesus Christ paid for me, the ultimate sacrifice, His blood, covering my sins, and paying the price for my redemption, my salvation. You know, what a sacrifice He willingly made for all of us; a gift by grace, you know. He's like, "I got you." you know. For me to think, hey, well, I'mma I'mma go be in charge. I'mma go show the world what what I got, cuz I got it, you know, and you know… okay, calm down. Breathe a little cuz guess what? You turned into a goat. You're starting to get all "greatest of all time on me" and that's my head going "Yeah, dude, uh, get over your cheap self."

You know, the last few weeks I've been depressed as can be. At least for me. Depressed as can be. Good Friday. It took Good Friday to remind me to get over my cheap self. Guess who made the ultimate sacrifice? Guess who really went through it? You think my little problems, my little concerns, confusions, you know, things not going the way I think they should be going about something, whatever. I think that that's not covered already by Jesus? We ain't ever gonna be able to approach what Jesus did for us. I could give every everything I got, everything I got, it's never going to come close to what Jesus has already done for all of us. So yeah, show up and do what God has asked me to do and just get out of the way. Get that ego. Get that greatest of all time ego that wants to be like, "well, you know, things should be like this cuz I'm trying." It ain't up to me how things turn out. It's up to me to just do what God says to do. So, part of getting over my cheap self and showing up to do a not-a-sermon on Good Friday; that's the least that I could do, not give up. So, here we are.

I'm gonna go back to my reading. Matthew, we were talking about that potter's field. Remember talking about that potter's field? The chief priest back at 27. Matthew 27. The chief priest took the silver pieces and said, "It is not lawful to put them into the treasury because they are the price of blood." and they consulted together and bought with them the potter's field to bury strangers in and then Jeremiah's prophecy saying "and gave them for the potter's field as the Lord directed me" and then going to that part where the place to bury strangers, and now, a couple chapters before that in Matthew 25 I'm going start again and try not to go on a tangent this time.

Matthew 25:31, "When the Son of Man comes in his glory and all the holy angels with him, then he will sit on the throne of his glory, and the nations will be gathered before him, and he will separate them one from the other as the shepherd divides his sheep from the goats.

"I'm the greatest." Oops… out of those two options, you want to be a sheep, follow Christ, or, go on saying "I'm the greatest of all time." That's how I think of it. Okay, we're going to be separating… or whoever does that. It ain't me. Forget that. I'd get so confused, that would never go well. But somebody, God, separating the sheep from the goats, the ones that are in submission following Christ, saying, "You show me what to do, I'll show up for you the way you show up for me, or, I'll at least try to follow you." And that's the only point to all of this, is following God, following Christ, shining His light, people being drawn to His light through me, through us, through the things that we're doing, and then following Him just like that. Then, it's just like a chain reaction of the love of Jesus Christ. Can you imagine anything more beautiful than that or more amazing and wonderful to be a part of something like that? To be a part of that. Not even "something like that." To be a part of that. Golly, you show up for that. I'm going off on another little tangent, but when I'm thinking about the sheep versus the goats, now I'm thinking about following Christ, being in submission. He is my shepherd. He's going to protect me. He's got me, versus "I'm the greatest! I'm the greatest of all time!" Yeah, I'll bring my cute little goat friends with me. little baby goats, but I'm gonna be a sheep. All right, I did it again, but I'm gonna keep trying to get through this without going on these little distractions.

So, he will set the sheep on his right hand, but the goats on the left. And the king will say to those on his right hand, "Come, you blessed of my father. Inherit the kingdom prepared for you from the foundation of the world. For I was hungry and you gave me food. I was thirsty, you gave me drink. I was a stranger and you took me in. I was naked and you clothed me. I was sick and you visited me. I was in prison and you came to me. Then the righteous will answer him, saying, Lord, when did we see you hungry and feed you or thirsty and give you drink? When did we see you a stranger and take you in? Or naked and clothed you? Or when did we see you sick or in prison and come to you? And the king will answer and say to them, Assuredly I say to you, in as much as you have done it to one of these, one of the least of these my brethren, you did it unto me.

So back to where, right after the part with where he talks about sheep and goats, verse 35 again, still in chapter 25 "…for I was hungry and you gave me food. I was thirsty and you gave me drink. I was a stranger and you took me in." That correlated in my brain; "I was a stranger and you took me in" to the potter's field. The chief priest took the silver pieces and said, "It is not lawful to put them into the treasury because they are the price of blood." And they consulted together and bought with them the potter's field to bury <u>strangers</u> in; the <u>strangers</u> that we were just hearing about. I was the <u>stranger</u> and you took me in; the prophecy of Jeremiah saying "…and gave them for the potter's field as the Lord directed me." All of this being connected, Jesus' sacrifice, paying the price for our sins. <u>The way we treat strangers is how we would treat Jesus. Jesus being the stranger.</u> Jesus paying the price for the <u>strangers</u>, <u>the unknowns in the potter's field</u>, the places, the place where they didn't know anybody, the person didn't know anybody <u>or they were the rejected of everybody</u>. The place where they buried Judas. "The last shall be first" if there ever was one; repenting after it was too late. But yet that part of the story had to happen for the rest of the story that was to come. And so, all of it is all of it is correlated. If you follow what I'm trying to say, in the way my brain ricochets between things and maybe this was something that was obvious to everybody from the beginning. Like I said, I learn slowly, and that's probably best, a little at a time is how I learn but <u>that potter's field being for strangers paid for with the blood of Jesus</u>. Right after Jesus was talking about <u>He is the stranger</u>. When did we… when did we see thee or feed thee or clothe thee or give thee shelter? He said, "As you have done it to the least of these, my brethren, <u>the stranger that you brought in, the stranger that you clothed, that you fed, that you sheltered, that you cared for, that is me. That is who I am bringing to you. To love the way I love you and the way that you love me, the</u>

stranger. The potter's field was paid for, for the strangers with His blood. Literally, the price of his blood; 30 pieces of silver, paid for the potter's field for the strangers, to be paid for a place for people who had no place paid for it, literally, with his blood.

I was thinking of all that, and thinking, you know, getting over my cheap self, and thinking, you know, my feelings get hurt that Purple Church of Jesus is tougher to do than I thought it would be. Mostly because, you know, I've got, I got a little tug-of-war going between my internal sheep and goat, going "it needed to be like this or needed to be more of that or needed to be less of that." Me getting all in there not being a sheep; being a goat, not like a cute little yoga goat, but you know, "greatest of all time! This is going to be the greatest of all time! This is exactly what the world needs and I need to bring it! God told me to! I'm going to! Now it needs to be like this and like that..." instead of just listening, saying, "Hey God, what do you want me to do next? How do you want me to do it? The rest is up to you. Whatever I do, I do cuz you asked me to do it. You said to. I'm going to do the best I can with what I got." Just like my Mom would say. The rest is up to God, not me.

There's a song I was hearing. I'm going to wrap this up. First, I'm going to read a little poem I wrote. You know, when I first started these not-a-sermons, I talked a lot more about, you know, I swore a bunch when I first started these and people got upset at me and they'd be like, "How can you talk about Jesus and be saying swear words like that at the same time? Blasphemy." You know, I think people's actions, what they do when they say they're followers of Jesus, then doing terrible things to… to the strangers… saying they're Christian while they're doing all the opposite of what I just read in Matthew 25, and saying they're followers of Jesus; that's the action. I think that's the blasphemy. Saying you're doing those things in the name of Jesus. I think that's blasphemy. Yeah, I don't swear like I used to, but when I started I sure did. You know, there was a point to why I swore so much; talking about spiritual abuse and how anything of a spiritual, religious especially, "Christian" even more especially, just feels so repellent and corrosive to people in the LGBTQIA community because we've been abused, spiritually abused through our whole lives. The culture is infused with this representation of LGBTQIA people as being "other than" anything to do with God, loved by God, holy in God, God living in us, God having value for us just like God does for everybody else, you know, and we grow up with that in our culture because of churches. I don't know where else to place the blame because that's really, it seems to be, the root of it. So, when I started these, I swore a bunch because that's how it feels to many in the LGBTQIA community when approaching something like this, because of spiritual abuse, and the deep-level PTSD that seems like it'll never leave us, because of that continual spiritual abuse. There's a point, but now I don't swear like that. Not really. I mean, not during my not-a-sermons. I'll still swear. You'll hear me swear in the world and I'm a human like everybody. But I don't think that that is reflecting of whether or not I'm following Christ as much as the actions that I take or the actions that people take in the name of Christ, doing the opposite things that Christ asks us to do. I think that's the blasphemy. I think what you do, the fruit, by the fruit you shall know them. What your actions are, says everything about what your intentions are; truly.

Anyway, I said all of that because this poem is called BFFFE means FFE; and BFFFE, as I used to say all the time in the beginnings of Purple Church of Jesus, I think of Jesus as my BFFFE meaning best friend for effing ever. BFFFE he's my Halo'd J. He's my BFFFE; best friend for effing ever. So, this poem is called BFFFE means FFE, for effing ever. This is the poem:

There is a reason
maybe even times two
why when it is said
you are losing your religion
it means you could be
going a little bit
cuckoo, like most
or at least like me.
Faith
in that last one thing
kept everything together.
But here's what to remember.
All of it, like all of it, all of it
can burn all the way down,
maybe even times two
to the ground
and guess who will still be standing
right in front of you,
looking right at you,
watching you see
Jesus.

BFFFE means FFE.

Even when I'm down, like, I don't know how to get through being that down. I don't even want to… I don't even want to get out of bed; finally get out of bed 3 hours after I'm not even tired anymore. Just lying there, not knowing what to do… get up, have a couple cookies, go back to bed for another couple hours… just pull the sheets up, you know… get out of bed again, go take a shower… should probably take a shower… go take a shower…get back in bed, get up again, thinking, I should probably go talk to some friends and let them know that I'm having a hard time. I can't do this alone. I need people in my life. Thank God for that. Thank God for that. And thank God there are people in my life that are these people for me and that we get to do this together. I couldn't do it without them. I couldn't. That's the honest truth, you know, getting back up out of bed and saying, "I need to see my people. I need to go talk with people. I need to be with people who understand me and who I understand, and we need to spend some time together and do today." And, through that process of that day, I'm not making up stories, this is how it's been for me lately a little bit; BFFFE means FFE.

Even in those times where I feel like that, guess who's there saying, "Hey, looks like you got yourself painted into a corner again, my friend. How about uh, just call out, call out for me, cuz guess what, I'm FFE." I'm in it. I mean it. And Jesus is saying, "I got you. I got you. I got you all the way." And when you feel like that… you know, a friend of mine, I'm going to say this real quick. Friend of mine, he has a tattoo of, you know, that Sistine Chapel where they've got the famous painting of God and Adam, like, touching fingers, you know? And, I never noticed this before I saw this on my friend; his tattoo on his arm. Name's Justin. Great guy. Tattoo on his arm of that, you know, God and Adam with the fingers. Everybody's seen it. Everybody's seen it. But you know what I never thought about until he explained it to me. I was like, that's really cool. I really love that tattoo. I think that's a beautiful painting and I love that depiction of God and Adam. He says, "Well," he says, "the reason why I wanted to get that is because I wanted to remember that in that painting, you'll see God and all of his angels just like coming clear through the clouds, you know, towards Adam, just like with his finger outstretched and Adam's like sitting on his… he's like this; he's just, he's got like his elbow up, he's just like, you know, squeaking his finger up, and God's all outstretched with reaching out while Adam's barely got his finger pointed towards Him, and God's touching his finger, you know. I had never even thought of it like that. I just thought, okay, well, Adam's just like doing what he's doing, and here's God and this is the beginning of life, God bringing life to Adam.

Justin says, "you know…" he said what I experienced too, I shouldn't speak for Justin, but what spoke to him from that painting, and what I get from that same painting now, is when we put the tiniest effort into it, reaching out to God, and God's got all of the angels with him coming through these big turbo-clouds like "I got you!" touching Adam on his finger after Adam gave the smallest effort.

I think about that. When I feel like I'm just like down and this is… this where I'm going to be forever; it usually feels like that when I get down like that. It's just like, okay, that's it. This is it. This is how I'm going to feel forever. You know that phrase I use; painted into a corner and stuck on stupid. It feels like that. Just like, dang, here I am. Got nowhere to go. I'm stuck. Stuck. Stuck. Stuck. If I remember… when I finally remember… "God, can you please help me? I'm stuck." and God says,
"I'm there! I got you!
I got you.
I got you.
I got you."

I'm glad I remember that. Doing the stuff that I need to do through the day to get through the messy-sad parts. reaching out to my friends, being there for them when they're reaching out for me, to me, helping them the way they help me, all of us getting through another 24 hours together. Guess what? I made it to Good Friday when I could finally remember, hey, maybe I can just get over my cheap self for a day. Remember the price that Jesus paid for all of us. The sacrifice he made for all of us, willingly, that he paid with his blood, 30 pieces of silver that bought the potter's field for strangers to have a place to be. That was paid for with His blood. That will always be; will always be.

There's this song that I really love. I don't know if I dare try to sing it. I probably shouldn't, but it's by a group called Elevation Worship called "Do It Again." I'm gonna try, but it's going to be terrible. So, now might be a good time to either pause or stop and then I'll end this not a sermon after that. So, if you just stop right now, you aren't going to miss any other great epiphany of anything. It's just me singing, trying to sing a song and then saying thank you. Thank you, God. But it's called "Do It Again" by Elevation Worship and there's a buildup about walls that are still standing, not falling down, etc. But then they sing… I'm trying.
I've seen you move. You move -I'm going cry more than I try- I've seen you move. You move the mountains. And I believe I'll see you do it again. You made a way when there was no way. And I believe I'll see you do it again. Seen you move. You move the mountains. And I believe I'll see you do it again. Back in that painted-into-a-corner again going… you made a way when there was no way. And I believe I'll see you do it again. As long as I can be a sheep and not a goat; "greatest of all time! I got it! I don't need anybody!" Follow Jesus. Remember to be a sheep. He's got me. He's got you. No matter how stuck you feel, no matter how stuck you're sure you are, no matter how sure you are that this is it, that's it. It's done. Guess who's got you? Guess who's got you. Just make that littlest effort… "…help me, Jesus." He'll be like, "Yeah! Come here!" He's got you. He's got you. He's got you.

I love you, God. Thank you, God. Thank you for being so reliable. Thank you for being in a place where I can trust my heart, my love; be safe in your arms. Thank you, God. No matter who or what of myself I bring to you, you're there for me. And I thank you. I thank you, God.

I'm not going to say 'happy Good Friday' because this is the saddest part of the Bible, but this is the part where it all happens. Blood of Jesus spilled willingly by Him for all of us. It's the ultimate sacrifice for all of us. Call on God. Call on Jesus. You feel like I described, or when you feel like you're having the best day in the world and you think that it's all because of you or you got this and you don't need anybody, call on God. Listen to God. Ask God what's next. And when it feels like there's nothing next, ask God what's next, because there's some… I'll see you do it again, you made a way when there was no way, and I believe I'll see you do it again again and again. I love you, God. Thank you, Purple Church of Jesus, for being a space where I can bring all my "gaaahhhh!"
I love you. Thank you. Oh, I have to say one more thing. I'm going to get a tattoo today; a little star. You can barely see a little faint, see it?
That's going to happen today in a real tattoo. There's a story behind it that I'll tell you about, but it's part of all of this. God's got me. And there's that little star showing evidence of that happened a couple days ago and it's going to turn into a tattoo today.

Peace and love and I say all these things in the name of Jesus Christ. amen.

I'll see you soon.

Purple Church of Jesus
greatness
greatness
be what is
for everyone for forever

The Immeasurable Greatness
The Immeasurable Greatness
April 5, 2026

All right, let's have a little… not… okay, all right, my babies. Is there a little place for us to to sit down and we can hang out for a minute? Oh my gosh, these bones. These old bones. Oh golly. Hopefully there's no spiders under here. Okay, AppleJacks, c'mon over here, buddy. I don't know if we're even on the TV thing, but we're going to try. C'mon. Are we on there? Hello!

Okay, just a quick-quick one for Easter. I don't have my glasses but I wanted to read because today is a great day. I'm here with AppleJacks and Mar-Lee. Hi, Mar-Lee! Hi, baby! Hi, baby! Happy Easter! Thank you, honey! Happy Easter, everybody. Just a couple quick things to say, Happy Easter. He is risen and because of Christ…

…hey, don't drink that water. It might have yucky stuff in there. The rain. Oh golly, my legs don't fit there. What am I thinking? Okay. All right, let's do this quick. I wanted to read a quick scripture from Ephesians. I don't have my glasses, so I'll squint like crazy. Ephesians 1:19. Let's see if I can read this. All right. Okay. Ephesians 1:19. Here we go. Read with me, Apple Jacks if we can.

And what is the immeasurable greatness all around us? Huh, babies? What is the immeasurable greatness of his power toward us who believe according to the working of his great might.
That's the scripture for today, and that was from church, earlier, and here's a little song, credit to Pastor Tauren Wells, who I'm sure wrote this song too, and I got to meet him today, so I wanted to give a little shout out to Tauren

Wells and give this a try because this song is really cool and AppleJacks is going to help me.

God of exceedingly, God of abundantly, more than we ask or think. Can you come over here AppleJacks? Lord, you will never fail. Your name is powerful. Your Word's unstoppable. All things are possible with You. Now, I get to do the drums. You going to help me? Here we go. Make way through the water. Walk me through the fire. Do what you are famous for. What you are famous for. I'm getting lost because I don't want to drum on my buddy. Let's start over. All right. Are you gonna help me? Make way through the water. Walk me through the fire. Do what you are famous for. Shut the mouth of lions. Bring dry bones to life and do what you are famous for. What you are famous for.
I believe in you.
I believe in you.
I believe in you.
I believe in you.
There is no fear. Cuz I believe, there is no doubt cuz I have seen your faithfulness, my fortress over and over.

Happy Easter. Worked up a sweat, doing all that mad drumming. All right. Peace and love forever. Look up that song. It's called Famous For. Tauren Wells. It's a lot better than the one you just heard from me. I guarantee it. But I also guarantee you're going to want to drum. You're going to want to be drumming just like I was trying to do. Yeah.

Look at that; old man gets up, that's worth watching. Happy Easter. Raised again with the power of Jesus Christ. Where is my… just like I said I would… I'll get you up close… there's my little star tattoo. I'll tell you a story about it later. Peace and love. I love you forever. Just like Jesus loves you forever; for ever ever ever ever ever. Happy Easter.

Purple Church of Jesus
greatness
greatness
be what is
for everyone for forever

Ain't Going For naked emperors Selling Lies and Fear

Ain't Going For naked emperors Selling Lies and Fear
April 13, 2026

Hey everybody, this is AppleJacks and pastor toddymanners.

Look at this mud he's got on his nose. He's a little cute little boy. Oh my goodness. You're covered in mud. Look at that smile. Look at that happy face. Come here. Get some happy face in there. AppleJacks, he's a good boy. He's a good boy. All right. Just want to say hi from our place. Hi, AppleJacks. There's my boy. There's my boy, AppleJacks. Applejacks. He's a good boy. He's a good boy. You got dirt on your tongue and everything, man. You're having a good day. We're both having a good day. It's hot. It's muggy. He's a good boy.

Just want to say hi and just a little-quick update. Um, what were we going to talk about, AppleJacks? Now I've lost my train of thought. Oh yeah; how the world has gone crazy. That part.

So just yeah, the world's gone crazy. But guess what? We follow One Jesus. Jesus Christ, son of God, our living Savior, living in our hearts. Jesus Saves. There goes AppleJacks. He's going to go play. So, keep that in mind. Keep that straight.

You know, you hear this craziness that's coming out of the nation's capital. I'll say it out loud. Why are there so many people that are afraid to say it out loud? People that say they love Jesus, and then they're afraid to call out the father of lies. Say it out loud. Gotta. Gotta.

Remember when, at the garden of Gethsemane, remember when Jesus was saying to Peter, he says, "Before the night is over, you will deny me three times." And Peter's like, "No way. Nuh-uh. I'm your number one." You know, if Jesus has a number one, "I'm your number one. I would never!" And what do you know… story's been told… before the night was over, sure enough, he denied Jesus Christ, out of fear. It was fear, survivalism, fear, whatever, fight or flight, all the human instincts. I mean, he was still learning, too. Jesus knew it would happen and he forgave him of course, but he was learning too, just like us you know. When he regretted it, immediately, he's like "I can't believe I actually denied Jesus three times just like he said. I would have never done that and yet I did."

Seeing how crazy things are in our nation's capital right now, every day is more insane than the one before that. People are so afraid to say anything about it cuz it's a culture of fear. Climate of fear.

What do they say about fear? "Fear knocks on the door, faith answers, and there's nobody there." I don't think that's in the Bible, but the idea of it is in the Bible. faith over fear. You know, lean into your faith. You got nothing to be afraid of. People are so afraid in this culture we've got right now, that terribleness can be happening right in front of us and nobody knows how to find their voice and say anything about
it. Paul denied Christ <u>three times because of fear</u>. Well, Paul would be able to tell you why, but I'll bet that's why; survivalism, fear, whatever you want to say about it, that happened even though Paul couldn't have imagined that being possible with how much he loved Jesus. "On this rock will be built my church, Paul" do I keep saying Paul? I mean Peter. He said that about Peter. And yet on the night

of Gethsemane, Jesus was taking on the sins of the world, saying, "If there's ever a time, why aren't my disciples able to stay with me?" They were falling asleep. Peter denied him three times. And we know his disciples were devoted 100% with Him. And yet in their human… is that the right word, frailty, or human weakness, or human-being-human, imperfect. You know on that last night they were falling asleep and denying Him as much as they loved Him.

You know what's going on in the world right now is insane; truly insane, led from the highest seats of power, worldly power. Big difference. It's got people afraid to say anything truthful about it. The emperor has got no clothes, marching up and down the street. Nobody can find their voice to say what-in-the-world is this lunacy going on; because of fear, survivalism, human imperfection, whatever the reason, not being able to say what we all see. Just remember though, you get One. You get One; follow One. If what you see coming out of world power leaders is incongruent with that One, choose the One. Of course, if they're in alignment, great, easy. But if one is going in the opposite direction, being the father-of-lies little play-thing on earth, you know what I'm talking about, if you can be honest about it. The father-of-lies is like, "Oh boy, this is a freaking circus parade that we got going on here and nobody can even say a word." Everybody's afraid. Fear knocks on the door. Who answers? More fear letting that fear in, or faith opening the door… ain't nobody there.

So, just want to say hi and say here's a moment in time with my buddy. Where's that good boy? That's my buddy. AppleJacks is such a good boy. Let's get you on there, bud. That's my friend. You got dirt on your nose cuz you're running around playing in the mud. Such a good boy. We're going to go play some more. Peace and love. I love you forever. pastor toddymanners, Purple Church of Jesus; it's going to take some form, probably out here in the woods after a couple months more of having brick-and-mortar. I'll probably let go of that place cuz I mean it's anywhere we go, right? And so, a little bit more of that, but we ain't going to go away, huh Apple Jacks. I love y'all and happy today, which is April the 13th, Monday.

I say all these things with love in my heart for you and for Jesus Christ, in the name of Jesus Christ, this beautiful place, our sanctuary, amen.

Purple Church of Jesus
greatness
greatness
be what is
for everyone for forever

To Know the Love of Christ that Surpasses Knowledge

To Know the Love of Christ that Surpasses Knowledge
April 20, 2026

Apple Jacks and pastor toddymanners, that's a good boy, good boy, that's a good boy. We're here at Purple Church of Jesus for Forever. We're going to be out here in the woods. There's little AppleJacks and me, being two little Sasquatches. AppleJacks and I just wanted to say hi and both of us did. Maybe if we go like that we can both get in here. Yeah. Golly. Okay, let's do it like this. That's a good boy. That's the Jesus I Know Now is a song I heard today by Brandon Lake and uh Laney Wilson I want to say. I'm not familiar with her. Although she sounded a lot like Dolly Parton. How about if I get down here by you, Apple? I'm going sit down here on the ground so we can be together. That's better. Get on over here. We're going to be hanging out here together a bunch for Purple Church of Jesus.

I heard that song today and it was really good. That's the Jesus I Know Now. It made me think about how, you know, we have this, I love you, buddy, personal relationship with Jesus Christ and how His love is unconditional and how fantastic it is to feel His love, feel the grace of Jesus Christ, to feel His salvation, to feel Him in our hearts, to be one with Him, for Him to be with us, for that to be a thing that gives us direction and purpose and a sense of meaning in this crazy life. All of those things that everybody who has a relationship with Jesus Christ knows intimately and is very likely the most important thing in their life. It is in mine. AppleJacks and me together, we're on this path with Jesus and discovery.

So, you know, I was thinking about this experience of creating Purple Church of Jesus, and how it kind of alienates me from some organized religions, who don't really know what to do with LGBTQ people in a humane way yet; they may think it is this love-the-sinner hate-the-sin stuff; Hi, buddy. There ain't no such thing as a barrier between us and Jesus, is there little AppleJacks? It isn't like "Okay, here's the conditions that must be met." It's unconditional. Unconditional love. The best kind. Yeah, like a puppy. Like the way the puppies are. The best. Yeah. Yeah. I love that. What a good example. Come on over here, my little friend.

But then, it's weird because even though we all have that same sense of unconditional love with Jesus, we put conditions on each other like, "Okay, but don't buy anything on Sunday or but don't get any tattoos or don't be an LGBTQ for sure." You know, "don't swear, don't drink alcohol, don't smoke, don't hang out with the wrong crowd, don't don't don't don't don't don't don't don't don't don't." Huh? "Unconditional… but don't… here's your list. Be sure that you don't, um… there's your list." There's my AppleJacks. He's way better to look at than me.

That song was really good to hear today. I listened to it a whole bunch of times; That's the Jesus I Know Now. Unconditional love Jesus. It was really great, I mean, listen to it. Brandon Lake and a lady who sounds like Dolly Parton and her last name is Wilson; Laney. Did I say it right? So, it's really-really cool and it made me think about like I started these not-a-sermons with how, you know, I kind of got stuck, in the middle of churches not knowing what to do with LGBTQs, i.e. me, you know, without them putting up some filters and without worrying about 'what am I going to do about that purple unicorn sitting in pew number 15 with his arms raised up to God in praise…' that was a big burp; that was a good puppy burp, …or from our LGBTQ community too, going, "Well, Christians don't really smile too brightly on our community." And so maybe pastor toddymanners has turned into a turncoat by becoming a born again Christian, and maybe he can't be trusted any longer and we're going to have to part ways. You know, I experienced both sides of that equation through this past year and it has been devastating. I won't lie, it's been heartbreaking. Absolutely.

Feeling the loss of the ground beneath me at some points. Like, what did I just spend all this effort trying to do; to bring to people? I Found It, in the process; and maybe that was the whole point. Jesus and me finding ourselves together through this past year. It's been transformative for me.

Maybe that's all that needed to happen. But in the process of trying to let go of stuff that I thought it was going to be, I ended up getting really depressed. Super depressed. And I did a not-a-sermon on Good Friday about getting over my cheap self, you know, and letting it be in my mind for at least a second, or hopefully more than one, about Jesus on Good Friday instead of my sad little depression trying to find direction, you know, finding Jesus. Forget about the rest. That was my not-a-sermon on Good Friday about the potter's field, but I think you can see in that how I was down hard. And you know, as a part of this… Besos are the best, thank you, Applejacks… as a part of this, I've been seeing a therapist and he said to me, “You know, Todd,” he said, "You look down; more down than I've seen you look before and I'm kind of worried about you." I assured him that I was not feeling suicidal, which I make sure to tell him because I don't want him worrying about me or anybody, you know, if I was feeling that down, I would say so. I'm not going to keep it a secret; and I was not… but I was down. He thought that maybe I could talk to somebody about getting on some anti-depressants. I trust him, so I did, and now I am. For Easter, pastor toddymanners started anti-depressants, like a little-teeny Easter egg. Now I have one every morning. I divulge that information because mental health gets a stigma. People kind of… it's one of those things like, oh, but you have depression? Oh, you're on medication? For some reason it's got a stigma. If I had high blood pressure or diabetes or high cholesterol or whatever, and I took a medication to manage that, it'd be no big deal. It would be like, "Oh, okay. Well, I hope that it's working for you." But for some reason, talk about mental health, talk about being on anti-depressants; that's kind of a thing people don't talk about. So, I wanted to talk about it. I just started it for Easter. On the day before Easter, I took my first one. Now, it's a couple weeks later. I'm feeling good. Not feeling like Mr. Euphoria, Mr. Manic, but I'm not randomly crying. I'm able to get out of bed. It got kind of rough there. I talk about it in the potter's field not-a-sermon, if you want to hear more about it. But I'm feeling better now.

Today when I heard that song, I thought, how awesome is it that some total stranger, whoever wrote that song, Brandon Lake and Wilson Laney. That's the Jesus I know. It ain't up to anybody else to say, "Hey, this unconditional love that is so great that we all feel, in love, it's conditional when it comes from me, and I cannot share the joy you feel towards um Purple Church of Jesus and the mission of Purple Church of Jesus because uh you know, I have to maintain my position of 'Christianity looks this way' or my sect, whatever it is, looks this way or you swore too much, you got tattoos, you're a big ol'… purple unicorn and we know what happens to those. They never made it on the ark for a reason.

So, I wanted to do a mini not-a-sermon, and read from some scriptures and read a little poem because I think that April is poetry month, right? Come here, buddy. What you doing? What you looking at? I need to reach my Bible. Can you help me get my Bible? I think it's under my hat. Maybe it's, well, there's my glasses anyway. I'll need those, with this teeny tiny Bible. We'll be done here soon, bud, and then we'll go walk. Okay, let's see if I can find it. There it is. Okay. Back to semi-organization. Are you gonna read this with me, Apple? Get this together. Let's get some Bible time. Thank you, buddy. Thank you. Good boy.

Okay. Ephesians again. We're going to go with Ephesians. Oh… my glasses are smeary now cuz of AppleJacks' besos. Yeah, that's you. You're my boy. Okay, here we go.

Ephesians chapter 3. wrote it down here versus 14 and 15 out here in the woods. What do you get when you cross a Snuffleuphagus with a Sasquatch? I don't know. But I think that I'm probably at least relatives of theirs; little love child. Ephesians 3:14 and 15. If you want to find your Bibles, now is your opportunity, or feel free to listen along because here we go: 13 and 14 of chapter 3 in Ephesians. 13:14 (exactly 13 minutes and 14 seconds into this not-a-sermon; wow, that wasn't on purpose) or did I say 14 and 15? Thirteen and fourteen is where we'll start. Well, I'm gonna go clear back to 11… 10… these are good… nine. Let's go to nine. Nine's a lucky number. We're going to start on nine.

Ephesians 3:9. Starting there and going to wherever. And to bring to light for everyone what is the plan of the mystery hidden for ages in God who created all things. So that through the church, the manifold wisdom of God might now be made known to the rulers and authorities in heavenly places. This was according to the eternal purpose that he has realized in Christ Jesus our Lord in whom we have boldness and access with confidence through our faith in Him. So I ask you not to lose heart over what I am suffering for you, which is your glory. For this reason, I bow my knees before the Father from whom every family in heaven and on earth is named, that according to the riches of his glory, he may grant you to be strengthened with power through his spirit in your inner being. So that Christ may dwell in your hearts through faith. That you being rooted and grounded …look at all these roots and ground… in love, …of course… may have strength to comprehend with all the saints what is the breadth and length and height and depth, and to know the love of Christ that surpasses knowledge that you may be filled with all the fullness of God.

Gosh, how beautiful was all of that? How powerful is all of that? I'm going to do it again quickly. Okay. I got Ephesians, chapter 3, and we're going to start on verse 9.

…and to bring to light for everyone what is the plan of the mystery hidden for ages in God who created all things …including AppleJack and me… so that through the church the manifold wisdom of God might now be made known to the rulers and authorities in the heavenly places. This was according to the eternal purpose that he has realized in Christ Jesus our Lord and whom we have boldness and access with confidence through our faith in Him. So I ask you not to lose heart over what I am suffering for you which is your glory. …this is Paul talking… for this reason I bow my knees before the Father from whom every family in heaven and on earth is named, that according to the riches of His glory, He may grant you to be strengthened with power through His spirit in your inner being, so that Christ may dwell in your hearts through faith. that you being rooted and grounded in love may have strength to comprehend with all the saints what is the breadth and length and height and depth. …All of it. All of it… And to know the love of Christ that surpasses knowledge.

You can't think your way through this.

That you may be filled with all the fullness of God. Now to Him who is able to do far more abundantly than all that we ask or think according to the power and work within us. To Him be glory in the church and in Christ Jesus through all generations forever and ever. Amen.

Thanks Apostle Paul. That was really good. I love that it talks directly about it; this love of Christ surpassing knowledge. Just feel that love of Jesus. That's the Jesus I know now. Let me see if I can, oh, I dropped my little piece of paper that had my little poem on it. This is kind of a …Hi, Mr. Apple Jacks. What'd you find over there? We're almost done here, bud. Just got to read this little poem. You wanna help me? You want to help me do a little poem here? This is the one we wrote last night. Here's a good boy. What's under that bridge? No spiders? Oh, don't drink that water. Well, that's fresh rain, so maybe it's okay. Hey, what's up, man? AppleJacks. Apple. AppleJacks. Come on. Come on. I don't know what's in that water, buddy. I don't know what's in there, but you're thirsty. I get it. We'll get you some water back at the car. All right; got a nice beso, let's do this poem and we'll go, all right.

Do not get caught up in a dance with confusion. There is absolute purpose... well, I'm going to start that over because it's the opposite of that.

Do not get caught up
in a dance with confusion;

there is no absolute purpose
in figuring on figuring out anything
while you are in faith
without any asinine needs
for reason
to begin with.
that constant tug of-war's
unpaid wages
consciousness prays about
getting its lights punched
into exxes
by way of subconsciousness
playing footsies
with awakening what will
please, pretty please,
turn every inch of groundwork
into blazing
destruction.

Yeah, that's about… kind of a '(being smirky) semi-poetic way of exploring'… letting go of having to know, letting go of having to understand, letting go of finding purpose. When you're in the Love of Jesus, that's all that matters. you get to the point of… let me get AppleJacks over here while we're making our final statements.

That's the point; not worrying about the point. Letting yourself go into subconsciousness. What's up there, bud? Here comes somebody. Got to go. All right.

Peace and love in the name of Jesus Christ. Amen. We got visitors.

Hey, how's it going?

Purple Church of Jesus

greatness

greatness

be
what
is

for everyone for forever

cross-legged floor puzzles with Jesus
May 7, 2026

Yeah, I don't know if this is working. It's dark out here. Hey, AppleJacks, come on. Come on, little AppleJacks. We're just doing an end-of-day walk in our sanctuary, and I want to say hi. I'll walk over here where my AppleJacks is. He's wandering. AppleJacks. Where's my buddy? Come on. Come on, AppleJacks. Here's AppleJacks. Come say hi, buddy. Come here. Come on. Come here, little friend. There's my Apple. You can't see him. There's my boy. You're a good boy. Wow, look at your glowing eyes, like you're here from a UFO or something. All right, you can go play. I just want to say hi. Quick hello from Purple Church of Jesus; pastor toddymanners and his good friend AppleJacks with the glowing eyes. Hi Applejacks. Thanks for the besos. What a good boy. You're a good boy. Just want to say hi real quickly and, I don't know what today is. I think it's May the um, do you know, AppleJacks? I think it's the 7th or the 8th in 2026. And we're saying hello from Purple Church of Jesus. Two little Sasquatches. Or a Sasquatch and a Snuffleuphagus; little bit of both.

I was thinking about, there's this game from back in the 70s. It may be still around. It probably still is. I don't look in the game section of the store much anymore, but I'll bet it's still around, some form of it because they do all those retro things now… AppleJacks, those glowing eyes are cracking me up… called Perfection. And they even had another version of it, which also may still be around called Superfection.

The thing about it is, even though you can't see this, except for those awesome glowing eyes on Apple Jacks, the thing about it is, it's like these little puzzle pieces, and you've got a minute, I think, to put all the puzzle pieces in the right places inside this little push-the-little-floor=of-the-game-down, if you want to think about it that way. There's this little inside push-down section, t's spring-loaded, and then turn the timer on. You got to turn it past 5 seconds, otherwise it doesn't work. So, you got to turn it past that, I think. Um, it's been a while. Turn it to a minute; and you got all these puzzle pieces. You got to hurry and put the right shape in the right little shape hole, if you will, in that little platform thingy that you just pushed down. You got to do it quick. Got to do it in a minute, like 30 of them pieces, or a lot, maybe more. And if you don't, whatever happens, at the end of that minute, that little pushed-down floor pops up and all the pieces come flying out and you jump and you laugh real loud, especially if you're a kid, and it's really fun and it's pressure and it's timed, you know, and it's fun, you know. I got to where I could just; I just memorized the whole thing real quick when I was a kid and I could do the whole thing in like 10 seconds, or about that; seems like. I would make it a challenge to see how fast I could do it and I'd get every piece in the right place within just a little bit of time and then I'd be like, "Ha, beat that!" to my brothers and sisters. Nobody could.

I loved that game so much that I wanted to get the Superfection version of it when that came out. Maybe they're both still out. I should look for them. Those would be fun games to play. That one, you had to put; it's the same idea. You push the little floor down, turn on the timer, you had all these pieces. However, they were each little puzzles like there'd be like a block that was broken into two pieces in different ways. You'd have to find the matching ones, put those little two pieces of each little block together, and put that little block on the little table thing that you had pushed down. There would be 16 of those little mini puzzles; put them together, put them on that little table before the timer runs out and it jumps up, pops up, and they all go flying and you jump and laugh and it's real fun and then you do it again and you try to do it faster.

You know, I was thinking about that as I'm walking around here in the park, Purple Church of Jesus outdoor version with my buddy AppleJacks, two little Sasquatches in the middle of the dark; not quite dark yet. We'll get home in time before dark. I was thinking about that perfection game while walking around here going, "you know, that's kind of just like life in a way. How we get anxiety, we get like, whoa, got to get these pieces in. I only got one minute or 30 seconds or something. Otherwise, everything's going to explode and it's going to pop up." And. you know, when you get to be a grown-up, and all that stuff pops up like that, you don't laugh like you do when you're a kid and you were like, "Ah, that's all great! Let's do some more! Let's do it again! I want to try again! Try again! Your turn! My turn! Your turn! My turn! Let's do it again! Let's both do it together and beat this timer!"
I was thinking about how, as a grown-up, that feeling of just carrying that around, like that spring-loaded floor feeling that you're trying to put your life on. All the little parts of your life, all the little different shapes that you never seen before; didn't know existed before. There are no names for those shapes, you know, and you got to find the right space to put those in because that timer is going like …hurry-hurry-hurry… uh-oh, it's not going in that spot! Uh-oh, it don't go in that spot! Where's the… try another piece… oh, yeah that goes in that spot. Good. All right. How much time we got left? Hurry. Ah, we're almost out of time. Only got five left. …hurry-hurry-hurry… then, KSHOOO!

You laugh-laugh-laugh when you're a kid. When you're a grown up, you're like, "Oh gosh, I can't figure out life. What’s wrong with me. What is wrong with life? Life's never going to work. Turn the timer again. Let's try some more.” After a while, that gets exhausting. But I was thinking about it like this, you know, and even with that second-level version, superfection, and you got to put the little pieces of mini-puzzles, put those all together real quick, then put that in there and then these, that in there, these, that in there. Except, you know, when you're a grownup, all those little puzzle pieces, they got little legs on them, you know, so they'll wander off that way. That one wanders off that way, someone picks one up, walks away, somebody else picks one up and eats it. You're like, gosh, I'm never going to get this puzzle together. But then, thinking about Jesus, of course, thinking about “how does Jesus figure into all of that, as a grown-up, when you're having all that anxiety and all those puzzle pieces are wandering off or somebody ate one and somebody stepped on one and somebody threw one at somebody they didn't like and now you got to go find that one. Meanwhile, that pushed-down floor is just going to pop up and everything's going fly and you have to start all over; if you can even try again. Bringing in Jesus; Jesus is like, "Hey, you know what? First of all, see that little timer on there?" He gets out his little Jesus-hammer… smashes that timer. There ain't no existence of that timer anymore. You got all of forever, you know. As one of my closest friends, partners together for a few years, for a few years in the early 90s, and he died of AIDS; that made me really sad for a really long time. But when we first started dating, I was anxious about “is this forever? Are we going to last forever? Is this true love finally? Forever?” And he'd say to me, “You know, that this moment existed at all, means that this is forever. This moment lives now forever because it existed on the timeline of there's-no-such-thing-as-time. Already; this moment will always be here. It'll be forever." He was reassuring me that no matter what happened, we're together forever. I'm reminded of that, especially every time it rains, because that's his Superpower; making it rain.

Thinking of that, Jesus smashing that timer, going… "You know, you've got as much time to put these puzzle pieces together as you want, and by the way, there is no wrong answer cuz I got you." Grace of Jesus; salvation through the blood of Jesus, him paying the price for our sins. You can try to put these pieces together, you know, and you can figure out the answers to some little mini-puzzles sometimes and put those little pieces together, but meanwhile, there's no timer on that. We're doing the best we can with what we got, the way my Mom would say. We're getting as many pieces that'll fit the right way or wrong way or upside down or right side up, inside out. We're learning as we go. I've never seen any of these shapes before. Where does that go? I don't know. Maybe with my friend, together; maybe I'll have some of the answers, my friend will have some of the answers, and maybe we can figure some of them out together. But, meanwhile, all those rascals that come around and try to pick up some of those pieces and throw them away, throw them at each other, throw them at me or swallow some, trying to sabotage my game; ain't going to, cuz guess what? Jesus already took care the whole thing. Smashed the timer, first of all, there-ain't-no-such-thing-as-time; ain't-no-such-thing-as-hurry in eternity because we're all getting there and we're all learning and helping each other there all along the way. including little AppleJacks here, trying not to fall asleep in this beautiful place.

Let me see. I'll give you a little look.
Sky night sounds.

Good stuff.
Thinking stuff's real important and kind of freaking out over stuff.
Come to a place like this.

Smash that timer.

Do the best you can with whatever shapes you got.

Get some help from some friends cuz none of us can do this alone. Maybe they'll have some of the answers that you couldn't figure out, that were right in front of you. Maybe you'll have some of theirs. Maybe the two of you or three of you or four of you or 20 of you together can go, "Hey, that part looks like that might go with that part… and it does… and you're like, "Hey, that was fun. Let's see if we can do another one." And that is life. We move through it like that, just today, just right now with your favorite buddy. AppleJacks and me together having a moment in our sanctuary. Purple Church of Jesus outside-version.

There's a little star way over there.
I don't know if you can see it.
I'm going to try
We doing this together, people.
You and me and Jesus.
Find him.
He'll help you smash that timer first of all,
so you don't have all that anxiety…
you just be like,
"Hey, this is kind of a fun little puzzle we're figuring out together."
Jesus saying, "Yeah, pretty cool, huh?"
Might be confused,
might go, what? None of these parts go together.
None of these parts have anywhere to go.

And then you get that "aha."
Just be patient with it because
there ain't no timer anymore.
Jesus took care of that.
We can figure this out as we go.

I love you, and this was a fun one to do. Just walking through the park with my AppleJacks, going, "you know what, there's that game back in the 70s that was so much fun."

We ain't going to freak ourselves out over this invented-timer. Let's get to where we could laugh like we did when we were kids; that thing pops up, and we're like, "well, we almost had it that time. Come on, let's do it again."

All right. I love you. Thanks for having fun with me out here at Purple Church of Jesus in the dark, trying to see the stars. I can see them. I don't know if you can, but you can at least hear the sounds. My little AppleJacks; time wake him up. We're going to go get some pizza.

All right. Peace and love, and I say all these things with love in my heart for you and for my Lord and Savior Jesus Christ. He died for all of us. Find Him if you haven't yet. If you have and you've forgotten or need to reconnect, do that, cuz wow, there's the answers for you, for all of us.

I love you and I say all these things in the name of Jesus Christ, my Lord and Savior…

… I think that there's a little star behind me…
was it?...
see it?...
…in the name of Jesus Christ, amen.

Purple Church of Jesus

♡ for everyone for forever ♡

Humble Donkeys Carrying Greatness
May 11, 2026

Hello, hello, and welcome to Purple Church of Jesus with my buddy AppleJacks. Today is the 10th of May, 2026, and I wanted to do a not-a-sermon today cuz I got this really cool tattoo today. See, I still got the wrapper on. Oh, he's peeking out. There he is. There he is. And I’ve got the tattoo stencil here too.

This is of a donkey from a nativity set made of Hummel statues, which is my Mom's favorite little figurine thing. She wasn't much of a collector of stuff. She didn't really need a bunch of stuff, but she loved Hummels.

After she passed away, I love you, Mom, a friend of mine, Chuck said, "Hey, I've got this Hummel nativity scene, and I don't want it if you want it” cuz he knew I was doing Purple Church of Jesus. So he's like, "This might be something you'd like. If you want it, it's yours." I'm like, "Heck yeah, man. Hummels were… that's my Mom, man. And they have it a whole Hummel whole nativity scene set? So cool!” So, the little donkey from that nativity scene; here he is.

Where's my little donkey? Do I need to flip him around? I don't think so. See, here’s my little stencil. I like to save these stencils. Ephesians 1:19. Remember when I talked about that one? I'm going to read it again tonight. I got that today, right here. Thanks, Mike. Thanks, my buddy, my tattoo buddy, Mike.

So, let's have a moment of meditation before I take the cellophane wrapper off of my new donkey buddy tattoo and we'll talk about him while AppleJacks has his little snack. I think he's already polished it off.

All right, let's meditate for a bit. Did you finish your treat? You ready for another one? All right, let's do this. He's a happy boy. He's a happy boy. I love you, AppleJacks. You're my good boy. All right, so my donkey, I haven't named him yet. But let's see. Where you going, Mr. AppleJacks? You going to go play some more? You got a toy over here? Here you go.

There he is. See all these raindrops? That's from my partner, Drew. His Superpower is to make it rain. So, it's raining a rain tattoo on my arm here. There's my happy dolphin, and that was a boy scout patch; I was in the fox patrol, so that's my little patch from the fox patrol from when I was a teenager. I thought it was really cool because then, right around the corner from my guy, my new Hummel donkey buddy, carrying his scripture Ephesians 1:19, is Pinocchio. I don't know if you can see him. You can't. You can kind of… there he is, with his donkey tail tied to a rock and his donkey ears flying up when he goes to the bottom of the sea to find his dad and faces Monstro the whale. He has already been to Pleasure Island, and he started turning into a donkey, but he escaped with his friend Jimmy Cricket. Even then, it wasn't before he had grown some donkey ears and tail. It was at this point, with a rock tied to his tail, that he started to think of somebody other than himself, and think of somebody else; his dad. He's like where's my Dad? So, he tied his tail to a rock and went to the bottom of the sea and went to look for him; went to face Monstro the whale. I love that that's right around the corner from my new Hummel nativity scene donkey tattoo, with all the rain from Drew and his Superpowers. Of course, Grover is here too, playing the banjo… anyway, enough about my tattoos for now.

The scripture that I tattooed on there was one that I read a couple weeks ago, on Easter. I'd gone to Easter service at the local church and they talked about Ephesians 1:19. I had my Bible with me, so I said, "Okay, I'm going to turn to Ephesians 1:19" and as I turned to that page, there was a little purple post-it note that I had bookmarked a page of my Bible with, from I don't know how many months ago; months before. Sometimes, I just write on little post-it notes and put them places cuz I write a lot and I put them on little notes to save for later. Anyway, I got closer and closer and closer to Ephesians 1:19, and as I got there, I realized, wow, this is exactly… this little post-it note is exactly on that page that they were talking about at church; Ephesians 1:19.

So, I'm going to read it again now. I read it on Easter, from outdoor Purple Church of Jesus on that glorious day. It says, "And what is the exceeding greatness of his power toward us who believe according to the working of his mighty power?" I'm going read it again. "And what is the exceeding greatness of his power toward us who believe according to the working of his mighty power?" with that little post-it from months ago right there. Isn't that cool, cuz I put the word "greatness"... I've got these little greatness hats, like with Jesus and he's wearing a purple hat says greatness in my own writing on there. And that's like: "greatness, reach for greatness." Instead of making greatness happen, be great. Be the greatness. "Greatness, be what is." One of my poems starts like that. "Greatness. be what is" kind of like when Gandhi would say be the change. It's like "be the greatness." Don't go make somebody else be your version of great. <u>You be great</u>. <u>Be great</u>. <u>Greatness</u>. "What is the exceeding greatness of his power?" There ain't nothing greater. "What is the exceeding greatness of his power toward us" …imagine that… "who believe" …imagine that... "according to the working of his mighty power."

It's all in faith. It's all in belief. Professing Jesus Christ as your Lord and Savior; the exceeding greatness of His power toward us who believe.

My little post-it note, that I had put in there a few months before, I had no idea that that verse was even in there about greatness. I had just been writing "greatness" on everything and trying to follow that. But then, written on the actual post-it note that I'd tucked in there from whenever-before, it says, "carry this inspiration with you." Carry this inspiration with you. I don't know what I was thinking about when I wrote this, but I just wrote it down on a little post-it and put it in my Bible at any page; and it to turned out to be page about greatness, which is exactly what I'm trying to accomplish with Jesus and Purple Church of Jesus. That's the little scripture that is on my little donkey, Ephesians 1:19.

I chose to get a donkey because, when you think about the story of Jesus; Mary. when she was carrying Jesus, when she was pregnant and going to Jerusalem, Bethlehem. She was riding on a donkey, you know. That donkey was carrying Jesus before he was born. Then, during Holy Week, what happened on Palm Sunday? He rode in on a donkey. Hi, AppleJacks. When he was riding into that last bit of his life, Holy Week, it was a donkey that took him there. So, I've got that donkey today from the nativity set that my friend Chuck gave me, honoring my Mom with the Hummel figures that she always loved. I love of that little donkey. My Mom always loved Jesus, my whole life.

AppleJacks, you're going to be right here with me, buddy, let's do this, okay, let's do this not-a-sermon together my bud; want to lay down? Do you want to lay down with me or do you want to just be a part of this? We can do that. We can do whatever you want, my friend. All right. So, AppleJacks and me doing this not-a-sermon together like we do. I'm going to tell you a little story about Jesus, okay Apple Jacks? Yeah. He rode a donkey on Palm Sunday. A donkey carried him into the beginning of his life and carried him all the way into town on his final week when he was crucified for us. So, donkeys are pretty cool. Why do you think they chose donkeys?

A friend of mine, Forrest, my brother in Christ, was talking about, you know, “have you ever seen how, if somebody rides a donkey, it's not like a smooth ride. It's not like riding a horse. Donkeys are a lot more rough of a ride.” Jesus rode in before he was born, rode in on a donkey and then that last week, Holy Week, Palm Sunday was on a donkey. So, Ephesians 1:19 is, to me, Jesus riding that donkey. You know, that promise in Ephesians 1:19 is the promise of Jesus, to me, and particularly in relation to what I've been trying to do with Purple Church of Jesus. It's all centered around him, just like he's centered around us.

Hi, AppleJacks; he's going to lay right there. You can't see him, but he's there. I wanted to talk about this because this week is Mother's Day and it's also nurse’s week and I was thinking about both of those things at the same time, and how this is also right after my Mom's birthday. My Mom is a big part of my life, every day anyway, but specifically at Mother's Day, my Mom's birthday, and nurses week all together like that; how one of the things that they taught us in nursing school, right from the very beginning, is to meet people where they are. Give the gift of self, the gift of being present. To meet people where they are; that we were going to be meeting people who were totally unlike us, who may be totally unlike what our value systems have always been, you know, and that they're there in need, with the importance of meeting them where they are, not being in judgment, but being there as a caretaker. That's really important; like, one of the most important parts about nursing. A person can tell if you're not really… if you're just like …hmmm… while you're taking care of them. A person who has been rejected by everybody can really tell whether you're really there for them or not. They really can; it's a moment when they see it. It's like, a sacred moment. It's holy. It's really cool. It reminds me a lot of what it was like when I was a full-time missionary, way back in the day.

I was thinking about that, thinking about my Mom, you know, and thinking about Jesus Christ, how Jesus is the Number One example of meeting people where they are. He doesn't arrive in some sleek set of wheels with white walls, you know, some high-octane muscle-motor... screeching His wheels to a stop, saying, "Jesus here!" No way. He gets here on a donkey, from before He was even born, here He comes on a donkey. Then, when He's facing His last week on earth as a mortal, half-mortal, getting ready to pay the price for all all of our sins; guess what? Did he have that muscle car yet? He'd spent three years preaching, talking to people from his heart, helping people to find the truth, helping people to find their way, healing people, bringing people back to life, literally; Lazarus.

You think he got some big fancy car for all that he did? No; riding in on a donkey. Jesus Christ, the son of God… in humility, our Savior.

So great. What an example. Start to finish.

It ain't about high-octane notice-me I'm-flash; I'm flashy. Meeting people where they are; who they are. Who did

Jesus arrive in judgment of? Nobody, except who? The hypocrites. The ones that were going to tell Jesus that he was breaking all the rules of the Bible. All the "holy writ;" hypocrites missed the whole thing. They're the only ones that he called out. He's like, "You know what, y'all? Scribes, Pharisees…" What did He say? No, not scribes. It was like Pharisees, hypocrites; they missed it. Everybody else, he's going to meet them where they are. Everybody else.

In humility, our Savior, Jesus Christ our Lord.

I'm really excited about this new donkey tattoo that I got. He hadn't got a name yet. I'll look and see if I can find a biblical name because that would be cool. I wanted to read Ephesians, wanted to read a verse from John, and a poem. Do a little poem. Sing a little song maybe. And then peace; see you again another time. I wanted to have a not-a-sermon <u>in</u> Purple Church of Jesus itself, rather than outdoors this time, because I'll probably let go of this place once the lease runs out at the end of July. I have some time to think about it. But I wanted to have another not-a-sermon sermon first, even though they're a lot of fun to have outside too. Huh, Apple Jacks. That last one was fun.

The scripture in John, at the very end of John, of the Matthew, Mark, Luke, John version of John. There is also one other verse; John 21:25. If you would like to get your Bibles, maybe you have some little post-it notes in there for your future-self to notice. Some really cool stuff. If you don't have your Bible, I'll read it for you.

John 21:25, and this is the New King James Version. "And there are also many other things that Jesus did, which if they were written one by one, I suppose that even the world itself could not contain the books that would be written.

Amen." Just like that, he says that; that's the very last verse of his book of Matthew, Mark, Luke, John. John chapter 21 verse 25. The very last thing he says is write about Jesus is, write more about Jesus.

There's no way to contain it; there'd be thousands and millions of books about Jesus if everybody wrote everything that Jesus has done for them. It's an encouragement to write about Jesus because this is just a small… bless you, bless you little buddy… this is just a small fraction. John 21:25. "And there are also many other things that Jesus did which if they were written one by one, I suppose that even the world itself could not contain the books that would be written. Amen." Just like that. "Amen." Thanks, John. That's a good one.

Write. Write about Him. Let's fill the world with books about Jesus and what He's done. Okay? Get started today. Just write a page. Just write a chapter. Just write one thing that you can think about with Jesus, what Jesus has done for you. Let's, let's write books. Let's fill the world with books about Jesus.

I'm going to read my… should I do my little song first? What do you think, Apple? Let's do it. I heard this song a few times today. Well, I played it a bunch of times. I heard it once and then I played it a bunch of times after that. So, this is a new song for me to try to play. It's not my song, but I liked it a lot. Kristian Stanfill; One Thing Remains. Kristian Stanfill, thank you for writing this song, One Thing Remains.

Okay, now this is gonna be terrible, but I haven't done a song for a while at Purple Church. Purple Church of Jesus, so I'm going to try to stretch out here with my doggy with my AppleJacks taking a nap right there by me, and let's give this a try. Let's get do the best we can with what we got. Here we go, kind of trying, okay, okay, the D chord is the hardest one. OW… I know, I'm sorry It's terrible. My song my… my singing voice is like… "What just happened to my ears?"

Okay. I'm sorry. Sorry, Todd, for insulting your singing. Do that, if you say something bad about yourself, you got to kiss your hand because my friend Desha taught me that, and I love it. If you say something bad about yourself, say, "I'm sorry" and kiss your hand. I'm sorry. There. I kissed my hand enough times. I'm going to try again. Here we go.

Now, forgive my singing as I also try to forgive my singing. It's higher than the mountains that I face. Yeah. Let's try doing two. I'm not chewing gum right now. So that's lucky for all of us. I'm gonna start over. And it's higher than the mountains that I face. And it's stronger than the power of the grave. It's constant in the trial. And the …I should just not even play the banjo… I should just sing. It's constant in the trial and the change. This one thing remains. This one, this one thing remains. Your love never fails. It never gives up. Never runs out on me. Your love never fails. It never gives up. Never runs out on me. Oh, love never fails. It never gives up. never runs out on me. Your love never fails. It never gives up. It never runs out on me. Your love.

Good thing it don't Good thing it don't run out. It would have been on the next freaking Greyhound bus, but it don't. It don't run out. And on and on and on and on it goes. It overwhelms and satisfies my soul. And I never ever have to be afraid. This one, this one thing remains. Your love never fails. It never gives up. It never runs out on me. Your love never fails. It never gives up. Never runs out on me. Your love never fails. It never gives up. It never runs out on me.

Your love never fails. It never gives up. It never runs out on me. Your love.

That was a solid effort. AppleJacks didn't run away. So, his love never fails. That's right, AppleJacks.

All right. Now, I'm going to just read a quick poem. No, I'm not going to say that one word because it'll make me have to kiss my hand again and I already did that three times, but I'm going to read a poem called Divine Contact that I wrote not too long ago. I wrote this about, you know; have you heard of that thing about a phantom limb? Like, if somebody has had their arm cut off, tragically, you know, or however it happens and um their amputated limb. whether it's their arm or a foot or leg or whatever, there's stories about how the person who that happened to will sometimes still feel that missing limb. They'll feel the arm that is not there anymore, or their hand, or their foot, or their leg or whatever, you know; like it'll itch or it'll hurt. It's not even there, but they've got this, I don't know what kind of nerve thing going on, that makes it feel like that's continuing. We've got these nerve paths that go all through our body. So, you can have something that hurts your foot and then you feel it in your shoulder. I don't know. It's weird. Derm… dermatomes… I don't know, something like that. It's all sciency. Anyway, I called this poem divine contact with that thought in mind, of, you know, somebody who has had an amputation and is still able to feel that limb, whether it's itching or burning or painful or just that it's there thinking that it's still waving at somebody.

Oh, there's a joke about that. Why did the guy who only had one hand cross the road? Why did the guy… do you know, Applejacks? Why did the guy who only had one hand cross the road? To get to the secondhand store! So that's, that's a little joke that goes with this poem, but this is called Divine Contact. It's more serious than that, but if you think of it like that amputated limb, and still being able to feel that limb even though it's gone. Think about that in relation to God and how we sometimes separate ourselves from God. He doesn't separate himself from us. He's always there. He's ready. Anytime we say, you know; I talked about it in my Potter's Field, not-a-sermon about the famous painting of the Creation, with Adam barely moving his finger towards God, and God going, "Yeah, I got you" with all of his angels and turbo clouds. We put the smallest effort forward; God's there. So, "Divine contact" is about, if we had lost contact with God and just felt… or in the case of some being excommunicated, kicked out of their churches, out of their families, out of their homes, you know, away from their friendships and people saying that was because of God frowning on us or rejecting us for whatever <u>their</u> reasons are or were… think of that in relation to God, and how sometimes, people tell people they don't have access to God or that God hates them or that God doesn't want to have anything to do with them. Sometimes, they end up believe those people, and they lose contact with God, even though God is right there the whole time saying to the others "Hey, you spiritual abusers, leave my kid alone. I love my kid. I'm there with my kid. I will always be there with my kid. How dare you tell any of my kids <u>who I love</u>, that I don't like them and don't want to be around them."

Gosh, don't ever be one of those people, cuz then, if you're somebody that that person believes, somebody that person trusts, or looks to for protection, for love, for direction, or if everybody around you is telling you all of that same stuff, you just believe… okay… well then, I guess that's me. Don't got… don't got God in my life… because I'm… I don't deserve it.

That's crap. Don't believe <u>anybody</u> who tells you that.

Getting separated from God, feeling that itch or burn or pain from that "separated limb," like you'd think of an amputated limb, think of that in relation to God and our relationship with Him; keep that in mind when I read this poem called Divine Contact after you've felt separated from God, still feeling that pull.

Divine contact

phantom limbs have their own
universally unseen inverses
the inside out
silent accompaniment of spirit
so very persistent
although
not with unresolvable
pain or plain itchiness
of what had been
chopped off or lost.
Just the baptism of fire,
bearing gifts,
God's own version of being
one or all three kings
bringing treasure to purpose,
establishing simultaneous
warmth and relevance in every direction
of His true spirit,
paying attention to confirming
this conversion of ours is
no longer porous

I ended the poem with the word "porous" as a kind of a play on words. P-O-R-O-U-S meaning, we're absolutely one. We are connected. There's nothing that is going to get in-between us; no longer porous. Also, the play on words being "poor us." This conversion of ours is no longer "poor us; oh, poor me." You know, I'd been separated from God. I'd been separated from my family. I'd been separated from my community. I'd been separated from blah blah blah blah blah, poor me. I don't mean to minimize that tragedy. I have gone through that and it's horrendous and I'm fortunate to still be alive because I felt like I had no purpose. I felt like every sign around me, every signal I was getting from every part of society, including "Christians", was that I didn't have a place here and that I should just go away. Um… so I had… yeah; I've spent my amount of time in that poor me place. Thank God for God. Thank God, God found me, saw me, said, "Hey, I'm not going to let people pick on you anymore because <u>you and me are together right now. And don't let go."</u> So, yeah, this conversion of ours is no longer porous. P-O-R-O-U-S.

Thank you, God, for helping me to write these feelings that I have been having as I have gone through being born again; saved. December the 6th, 2025, and continuing Purple Church of Jesus. Even though it's just AppleJacks and me, honestly, that purpose is still here. It doesn't matter if a thousand people come through that door or if it's AppleJacks and me. We continue to bear testimony of Jesus Christ our Lord and Savior for anybody who will hear. I will be a street corner preacher standing on a soap box. Not an actual soap box, but I do have this old, wooden 7-Up box. I'll have to reinforce it so that I don't just break through it, but yeah, I can see that. You know, I'm here. This is the equivalent of doing street-corner preaching in the modern-day, I guess, preaching that Jesus Saves. I'm here to talk about Jesus. Jesus Christ being my Lord and Savior. He died for all of our sins; died for us and gave us the grace of forgiveness, salvation through His blood for us, for all of us.

We just follow Him.
He'll show us what to do.
Follow him.
Follow Jesus.
You get One.
Figure out who you're following.
Follow Him for forever.
You won't even know when this life is over because we'll just be following Him.
We won't even see a shadow behind us.
It'll just be where are we going? Jesus.
Just keep on going forward.
The rest will be figured out.

All right. So, that's AppleJacks and me for today. Purple Church of Jesus. May the 10th, the day I got my donkey tattoo, giving a ride to Ephesians 1:19. I need to figure out a name for my donkey. "Ayir." His name is Ayir. There he is, getting rained on by all of the Superpower of Drew-man, right next to Pinocchio who already grew his donkey ears.

I love you. I love Jesus Christ my Savior. I love my AppleJacks. And I'll see you soon. I say these things in the name of my Lord and Savior Jesus Christ …find Him…find Him…find Him. You'll know what I'm talking about. You'll try singing songs with your corny voices too. Well, I'm sure you have really nice voices about Jesus, because you just can't contain it. It's going to happen. That's the joy. That's the joy. Be a little jacko'lantern for Jesus. Let that light shine out. Don't hide that. He told us. So, all right. I love you very much. Keep together, with Apple Jacks and me. I'll see you soon. I say these things humbly in the name of my Lord and Savior Jesus Christ. Thank you God. Thank you for this beautiful day. Thank you for everything in my life, amen.

I'll sing another song next time. I'll maybe practice a little more, little less, a little more. I don't know.

peace

Sarah B.
& Rita

It is no longer
I who lives, but
Christ who lives in me
Gal 2:20

Your Friend,
Forrest
12/26

B.T. / Shorty
3/10/20
Shorty

Testimony from Bryan, my true brother in Christ:

God loves you!
He truly does. All He needs to change your life for all eternity is an earnest, committed heart to know Him. If you believe there is a God, or even if you have a small, quiet suspicion that there just might be, then why not get to know Him, personally, intimately; seek Him, and do all you can to meet Him? You have nothing to lose, and everything to gain.

He's waiting for you. His Son Jesus Christ made a way to Him for you, to have everlasting life and a fulfilling, purposeful, blessed life in this world. He is real. He is powerful! He is love. What are you waiting for? His promise to you is "seek and you will find. Knock, and the door will be opened to you." His glory awaits in you. What are you waiting for?

Testimonies from my Missionary Family, Elder Aaron and Elder Cade:

The Spirit is something that we take for granted. We cannot have a real relationship with God unless we can recognize the Spirit. That same Spirit that prompts us to repent, that prompts us to act, that prompts us not to act, that prompts us to love… gives us life. I love the story of Ammon and King Lamoni. King Lamoni recognizes the remarkable service Ammon had been to his kingdom and to his flocks. The king recognizes the Spirit in Ammon, as he proclaims "Surely, this is more than a man" (Alma 18:2). The Gift of the Holy Ghost allows us to become more than a man. We literally acquire a part of heaven. When we serve and love as Jesus Christ would, we walk with Him. I have to make that choice daily, but the Spirit enables me to make that choice. Every morning I remind myself:
"TODAY IS THE DAY THAT I WALK WITH GOD!"
Elder Aaron Hoggard, Arizona Mesa Mission

A testimony is an account based on personal experiences and beliefs. I have an earnest testimony of the Savior Jesus Christ. As a missionary for The Church of Jesus Christ of Latter Day Saints, I testify of the Savior each and every single day. I know that He lives. I know that He sees me. Christ is the way that we are able to connect with our Father in Heaven. Because of Christ, we are enabled to change. Many people can become caught up in life and the ways of the natural man. There is temptation on every block. Often times, it can become easy to fall into these traps of temptation that are set. Some may be easier to get out of than others. Some may feel impossible to get out of. The simplest and most joyful message on the earth today is that we will always get out if we choose to follow Jesus

Christ. Choosing to follow Him is choosing to not walk alone, even when it seems to be the loneliest of times. Choosing to follow Christ is choosing to have joy. Some may decide it's easier to take the route of life alone. As we do this, we become prone to running into dead ends. Prone to fall in the traps of life, and never get out. But even if we don't choose Christ, He always chooses us. Even if we decided to take a different route than His, He will still follow close behind. If we are stuck in a trap and can't get out, He will still stand by our side. The joy comes when we decide to turn to Him. To reach out and ask for His help. Christ will never abandon us. He begs us to choose Him. As we choose Him, He will provide the strength necessary to break out of the traps of life. I love my Savior. Choosing to follow Him will always be the best decision I've made in my life. Nothing is possible without Him. He loves you. Choose to love Him. In the name of Jesus Christ, Amen.
Elder Cade Wilkinson, New York, New York City Mission

photo credit: Kelly Johnson,
my brother in Christ

YOU ARE
Beautiful

BFFFE means FFE

there is a reason
maybe even
times two why when
it is said
you are losing
your religion, it means you
could be
going a little bit
kookoo, because like most
or at least
like me, faith in that last,
one thing, kept
everything together... but,
here is what
to remember: all of it;
like, all of it all of it can burn
all the way down,
maybe even times two
to the ground and guess who
will
still
be standing right in front of you,
looking right at you,
watching you see,
JESUS.

Halo'd J, AppleJacks,
Ayir the donkey and
pastor toddymanners
greatness
greatness
greatness
greatness
Jesus ♥ you
BE
WHAT
IS
for
Forever

JESUS
SAVES

AppleJacks and pastor toddymanners for Forever

...in the name of

Jesus
Christ...

amen.

...on that first, most famous day of rest,
God created dog smiles;
and God could see
that it was good
and God rested.

www.ingramcontent.com/pod-product-compliance
Lightning Source LLC
LaVergne TN
LVHW010544110826
845149LV00003B/559

* 9 7 8 1 9 6 5 5 3 5 2 2 6 *